Eyewitness
VICTORIANS

Kitchen utensils

Ironworker

Punch and Judy puppets

Queen Victoria's parasol

Mangle

BOVRIL

Wall advertisement

Victoria and Albert's wedding

Salvation
Army bonnet

Memorial
newspaper

Eyewitness
VICTORIANS

Written by
ANN KRAMER

Mrs Beeton's *Book of
Household Management*

Geometric shapes

Christmas card

Portmanteau
and hatbox

Playing
cards

Ruby
lustre tile

DK

A Dorling Kindersley Book

Egg and
dart cornice

Servant's bell

LONDON, NEW YORK,
MELBOURNE, MUNICH, and DELHI

Project editor Claire Bampton
Art editor Lesley Betts
Picture research Melissa Albany,
Marianna Sonnenburg, Helen Stallion
Photographers John Chase, Andy Crawford
Illustrators Adam Abel, Lee Montgomery
Editorial consultant Aan Wilkinson

Paperback Edition
Editors Kitty Blount, Susan Malyan
Art editors Rebecca Johns, David Ball
Managing editors Andrew Macintyre, Camilla Hallinan
Managing art editors Jane Thomas, Martin Wilson
Publishing manager Sunita Gahir
Production editor Hitesh Patel
Production controllers Jenny Jacoby, Pip Tinsley
Picture research Sarah Powell, Rose Horridge,
Myriam Megharbi, Emma Shepherd
Jacket designer Smiljka Surla
Jacket editor Rob Houston
Wallchart Neville Graham, Sue Nicholson

This Eyewitness ® Guide has been conceived by
Dorling Kindersley Limited and Editions Gallimard

Hardback edition first published in Great Britain in 1998
This edition published in Great Britain in 2003, 2008 by
Dorling Kindersley Limited, 80 Strand, London WC2R ORL

10 9 8 7 6 5 4 3 2 1
001 – ED699 — July/11

A CIP catalogue record for this book is available from the British Library.
ISBN 978-1-40537-322-7

Colour reproduction by Colourscan, Singapore
Printed and bound by Toppan Printing Co. (Shenzhen) Ltd, China

Discover more at
www.dk.com

Child's
box toy

Family
photographs

City of
London fire
bucket

Lemonade and
beer bottles

Home remedies

Contents

Sheet music

Commemorative fan

Queen Victoria's reign

QUEEN VICTORIA CAME TO the throne in 1837. She ruled for more than 63 years and is the longest-reigning British monarch. Her two immediate predecessors had been something of a disgrace and Victoria was determined to restore dignity to the throne. She was active in state affairs and her family life, with her beloved husband Albert, provided a model for the nation. Her reign spanned a period of enormous change: Britain had the world's biggest empire, the largest navy, and the most modern industries. When Victoria died in 1901, she was a symbol of British greatness and much loved. Her reign is known as the Victorian Age and British people of the time as Victorians.

A princess's life

The young Princess Victoria grew up in Kensington Palace, London. Her mother was over-protective, and her up bringing was strict. She was constantly supervised, and had few companions. Later, she described her childhood as "rather melancholy".

Becoming Queen

When she was 10 years old, Victoria learned that she was heir to the throne. She said "I will be good". She was only 18 years old when she became Queen, but took to her duties with enthusiasm and determination. Within hours, she attended her first official meeting with leading politicians.

DUTIES AS QUEEN
Victoria was a constitutional monarch. This means she was not allowed to decide affairs of state. Real political power lay with Parliament, and much of her work was ceremonial. But Victoria worked closely with her ministers, and was particularly interested in the progress of the British Empire.

MARRIAGE TO ALBERT
In 1840 Victoria married her German cousin, Albert. She was devoted to him, describing him as her "dear Angel". For 21 years, until he died, he was her closest companion and adviser, and taught her much about political matters.

Queen Victoria's sketchbook

Princess Victoria's music book

Victoria sketched people and places from memory

Sketch of the Scottish Highlands

Queen Victoria (1838) by Sir George Hayter

The sceptre is a symbol of authority

Victoria, was only 1.5 m tall, but had an imposing personality

HOBBIES AND INTERESTS
Throughout her early and married life Victoria loved music, dancing, sketching, and later took up horse riding. When she was 13 years old she began to keep a diary, which she continued until her death.

QUEEN VICTORIA 1819–1901

Victoria's life spanned most of the 19th century, and her name is closely associated with the age. Through her children and grandchildren, she was connected to almost every European royal house (see p. 42).	*1819* **BIRTH** 24th May: Victoria is born at Kensington Palace, London. When her father, the Duke of Kent, dies, her mother, and adviser Sir John Conroy, supervise her upbringing.	*1837* **QUEEN** 20th June: Victoria becomes Queen following the death of her uncle, William IV. She is his only heir. A year later, aged 19, Victoria is crowned at Westminster Abbey, in London.	*1840* **MARRIAGE** 10th February: Victoria marries her German cousin Albert, Duke of Saxe-Coburg-Gotha. They are happily married for 21 years.

Crown

Crown jewels

Victoria in her coronation robes, aged 19

FAMILY LIFE
Victoria and Albert had nine children – five daughters and four sons. Victoria disliked pregnancy but saw it as her duty to produce heirs to the throne. She valued family life and, royal duties allowing, she and Albert spent as much time as possible with their children. Their close-knit home life impressed the British public. Victoria had 37 grandchildren, many of whom married into royal houses across Europe.

Of Victoria's nine children, three died before their mother: Alice, Leopold, and Alfred

Prince Albert

Queen Victoria

Queen Victoria and Prince Albert with their nine children

STATESMEN AND VICTORIA
Ten prime ministers held office during Victoria's long reign (see p. 42). One of her great favourites was Viscount Melbourne who was prime minister when she came to the throne. He gave her sound political advice, and friendship.

see p. 42

Victoria held her first Privy Council only a few hours after becoming Queen

Balmoral Castle was Queen Victoria's favourite home

CASTLE RETREAT
When Victoria became Queen, she moved into Buckingham Palace, but never thought it suitable for children. During the 1840s, she and Albert bought and restored two family homes: Osborne House on the Isle of Wight, and Balmoral Castle in the Scottish Highlands. After Albert's death, Victoria spent much time at Balmoral, grieving in the company of her closest servant, the Scotsman John Brown.

1861
WIDOWHOOD
Albert dies from typhoid. Victoria is heartbroken and retires from public life for 13 years. The British people resent her absence. She wears black for the rest of her life.

1876
EMPRESS OF INDIA
From the early 1870s, Victoria resumes public duties, encouraged by Prime Minister Disraeli. He involves her in foreign affairs, and, in 1876, Parliament gives Victoria the title "Empress of India".

1897
DIAMOND JUBILEE
Queen Victoria, now in a wheelchair and suffering from rheumatism, celebrates 60 years on the throne. She is at the height of her popularity, and connected to every royal house in Europe.

1901
DEATH
22nd January: Victoria dies at Osborne House, aged 81. She is buried, next to Albert, at Windsor Castle, Berkshire. Britain and the Empire mourn her death.

First industrial nation

By 1837, BRITAIN WAS undergoing extensive industrial expansion. The Industrial Revolution had begun in the late 18th century, and with it came new machinery, and new sources of power, particularly steam. Steam-driven machinery could do the work of many people, and the manufacture of goods moved into factories enabling mass production. New industries emerged, creating new products and different types of work (see p. 43). The pace of change varied according to industry and region, but during the Victorian period it intensified, transforming British society and making Britain the world's first, and most powerful, industrial nation.

The Shingling Hammer
by William McConnell

Raw materials

Coal and iron made the Industrial Revolution possible. Coal furnaces boiled water to produce steam, which drove new machines. Coal stimulated iron and steel production and powered locomotives and ships. The coal mined in Britain soared from 30.5 million tonnes in 1836 to 150 millions tonnes in 1890.

Iron ore

Britain was rich in coal

Ladle to skim impurities from molten iron

Wrought iron rod, shaped by hammering or beating

Iron bars

Iron was used to make new machinery

Iron working

In 1828, the development of a hot-blast furnace, which used coal instead of charcoal, made iron working cheaper. In 1839, James Nasmyth invented a powerful steam-driven hammer that shaped iron with extraordinary precision. These two innovations helped produce new goods from railway tracks to machinery.

STEEL AGE

Steel, made from pig iron with added carbon, is stronger and less brittle than cast iron. In 1856, Henry Bessemer invented a converter that produced steel easily, by applying a hot blast to molten pig iron. In 1866, the Siemens open-hearth steel furnace made it possible to produce steel in bulk. These developments created massive new industries: steel, engineering, and shipbuilding. From the 1860s, ships, boilers, and huge structures such as bridges, were made from steel.

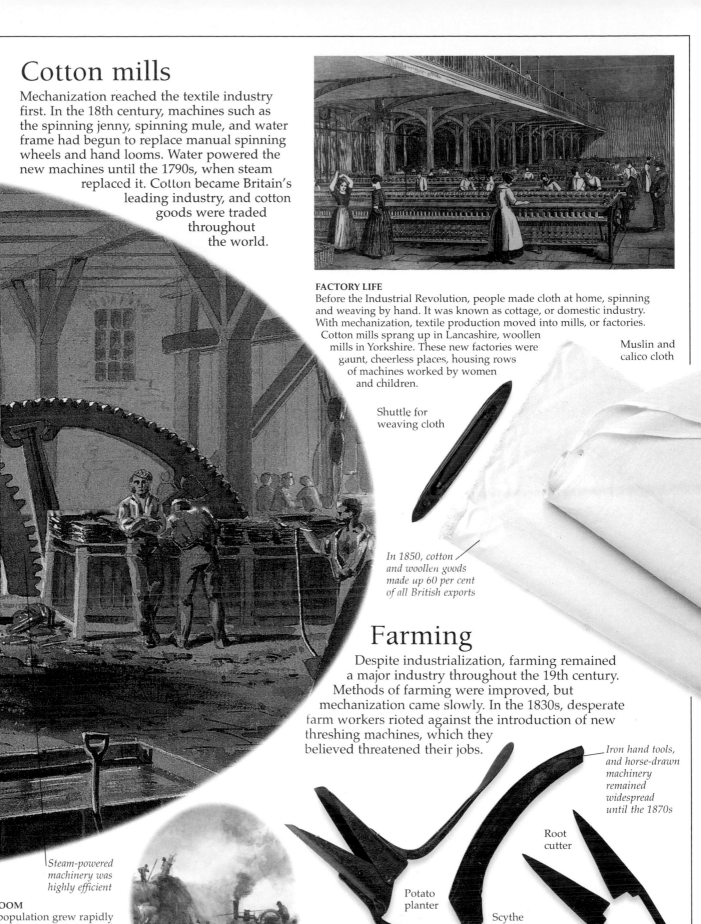

Cotton mills

Mechanization reached the textile industry first. In the 18th century, machines such as the spinning jenny, spinning mule, and water frame had begun to replace manual spinning wheels and hand looms. Water powered the new machines until the 1790s, when steam replaced it. Cotton became Britain's leading industry, and cotton goods were traded throughout the world.

FACTORY LIFE
Before the Industrial Revolution, people made cloth at home, spinning and weaving by hand. It was known as cottage, or domestic industry. With mechanization, textile production moved into mills, or factories. Cotton mills sprang up in Lancashire, woollen mills in Yorkshire. These new factories were gaunt, cheerless places, housing rows of machines worked by women and children.

Muslin and calico cloth

Shuttle for weaving cloth

In 1850, cotton and woollen goods made up 60 per cent of all British exports

Farming

Despite industrialization, farming remained a major industry throughout the 19th century. Methods of farming were improved, but mechanization came slowly. In the 1830s, desperate farm workers rioted against the introduction of new threshing machines, which they believed threatened their jobs.

Iron hand tools, and horse-drawn machinery remained widespread until the 1870s

Root cutter

Steam-powered machinery was highly efficient

Potato planter

Scythe

FARMING BOOM
The British population grew rapidly from 1801 and the demand for fresh produce caused a farming boom in the 1850s. Landowners and farmers made huge profits, but farm labourers lived in dire poverty throughout the 19th century. Many eventually left to work in the new industrial towns.

Steam-powered threshing machines reduced the work available for farm labourers

Coming of the railways

Transport of all kinds – trains, buses, and ships – developed rapidly during the Victorian period, but it was the arrival of the railways that made the biggest impact on British society. By moving raw materials and finished goods quickly around the country, railways boosted the economy, and stimulated the iron and steel industries. Railways speeded up trade, provided employment, encouraged the growth of towns, and opened up a new world of travel to millions of people. Starting in the 1840s, railway "mania" gripped the country. In 1843, there were 3,123 km of railway track; by 1870, the railway network covered more than 20,920 km (see p. 43). Goods, people, mail, and ideas were travelling faster than ever before.

A GREAT ENGINEER
One of the greatest Victorian engineers was Isambard Kingdom Brunel. He created the Great Western Railway, and planned Clifton Suspension Bridge, over the River Avon. He also designed the *Great Western*, the first trans-Atlantic steamship, and the *Great Britain*, the first screw-propelled ocean steamship.

Isambard Kingdom Brunel

Steam power

In 1803, the first steam railway locomotive was invented. Coal burned in a boiler and heated water to produce the steam that powered the engine. Trains were powered by steam until the 1890s.

Gases from the firebox left the locomotive via the chimney

Steam whistle

Columbine steam locomotive

Steam drove the pistons back and forth. These were connected to a rod and crank

Piston, linked to rod

Rod drove wheels around

Navvies worked with picks, shovels, and barrows

BUILDING THE RAILWAYS
Railway pioneers, such as George Stephenson and Isambard Kingdom Brunel, planned and built Britain's railway networks. With no modern digging machines, they hired people to carve up the land. Huge gangs of skilled workmen, known as navvies, did the back-breaking and dangerous work of constructing tracks, bridges, tunnels, and embankments.

Workman's shovel

Workman's pick

THE NAVVIES
Some 250,000 navvies built the British railways. They took their name from "navigators", workmen who had built the canals in the 18th century. Navvies worked at amazing speed, shifting as much as 20 tonnes of earth daily. They lived rough lives in shantytowns beside the tracks.

19TH-CENTURY TRANSPORT

Before the 1830s, people travelled long distances in horse-drawn transport. During the Victorian period, forms of public transport changed dramatically.

1850s
DOUBLE-DECKER BUSES
In 1829, the first horse-drawn omnibus, or bus appeared on the London streets. By 1850, buses had become double decked with open tops, and by 1902 motor buses had replaced them.

1863
FIRST UNDERGROUND
The world's first underground railway – the Metropolitan Line – opened in London in 1863. Steam engines pulled carriages, which ran through roofed trenches.

RAILWAY "MANIA"

Most of Britain's railways were built during the 1840s and 1850s. They developed in a haphazard way. There was no national plan. Instead, private individuals built separate lines, forming companies to raise money. Shareholders then shared in the profits. During the railway "mania" of the 1840s, people made profit from investing in the railways. Individuals, such as George Hudson, the "Railway King", who founded the North Eastern Railways, made fortunes. By the 1850s, the boom, and profits, were over.

Great Western Railway station master's hat

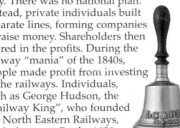

Lancashire and Yorkshire Railway whistle

London Chatham, and Dover Railway insignia

HOLIDAYS BY TRAIN

Many Victorians distrusted the new trains, but in 1842, Queen Victoria made her first train journey. Soon, increasing numbers of people were using trains to travel to work, and go on holiday. Seaside resorts such as Ramsgate, Margate, and Blackpool were developed. With cheap fares, even the less well-off could go to the seaside.

Railway stations

Stations appeared as railway lines arrived in different cities. Many of the main stations were huge, glass-roofed constructions, full of smoke and steam. This painting, The Railway Station (1853) by English artist William Frith, captures the excitement and bustle of a Victorian station.

By opening the regulator valve the train was propelled forwards or backwards

Coal burned in the firebox

The train driver stood here

Coal regulator to stem the flow of coal

Coal was stored in this truck

1868

Coupling rod

First-class compartment

Train ticket

TRAVELLING CONDITIONS

Early trains were uncomfortable, and could be dangerous, as signalling was basic, and speeds were uncertain. Third-class carriages were little more than boxes on wheels. Some passengers used hot-water-filled boxes as foot warmers. Gradually conditions improved. In the 1870s, upholstered seats were fitted. Steam heating came in 1884, and restaurant cars in 1892.

COST AND SPEED

Train travel was faster, and cheaper, than long-distance horse travel. From 1844, third-class travel cost one penny a mile (1.6 km), and all passenger trains had to keep to an average speed of about 20 km/h. By 1895, speeds had reached an average of 112 km/h.

Ticket clippers

1870
PENNY-FARTHING
The first pedal bicycles appeared in 1839. Later, "penny-farthings" with different-sized wheels appeared. They were difficult to ride, but popular. By 1885, bicycles had equal-sized wheels, and a safety chain.

1885
ELECTRIC TRAMCAR
Horse-drawn tramcars for public transport came into use in the 1860s. They ran on steel rails. Later steam replaced horses, and in 1885, the first electric tramcar was used in Blackpool.

1896
MOTOR TAXICAB
The first successful car was made in Germany in 1885. It looked like a horseless carriage. Gradually this new type of transport appeared in Britain. Battery-driven taxicabs were used, briefly, in London.

The Great Exhibition

B<small>Y</small> 1815 B<small>RITAIN WAS</small> the world's greatest industrial nation. The country traded freely with the rest of the world and enjoyed a period of extraordinary economic growth, which lasted until the 1870s. Britain exported goods worldwide and became known as "the workshop of the world". To celebrate and promote the successes of the Industrial Revolution, Prince Albert suggested and planned the Great Exhibition. Held in 1851, it was the world's first international exhibition and a remarkable monument to Victorian achievement.

Royal spectacle

On 1 May 1851, Queen Victoria and Prince Albert opened the Great Exhibition. It was held in London's Hyde Park in a specially built "Crystal Palace". The six-month exhibition was an outstanding success. One journalist described it as "the grandest spectacle the world has ever witnessed".

INSIDE THE EXHIBITION
The main exhibition hall in the Crystal Palace was vast. It covered 9,300 sq m and its glass-topped ceiling was 19 m high. A central area, full of statues and a fountain, led to display stands on different levels. More than 100,000 exhibits were on show.

A Crystal Palace

Joseph Paxton

The centrepiece of the Great Exhibition was the exhibition hall itself. Designed by architect Joseph Paxton, it was made from iron and glass, and nicknamed "Crystal Palace". Later the hall was moved from Hyde Park to south London, where it survived until 1936.

Great Exhibition season ticket

RAILWAY EXCURSIONS
The new railways ran special excursion trains from industrial towns to London, so that workers could visit the exhibition. Some people went several times, using a season ticket.

The hall consisted of prefabricated "units", made in factories, and taken to Hyde Park by train

Units were bolted, screwed, or slotted into place

The building was 550 m long and 140 m at its broadest point

The Crystal Palace was the first large public building to contain public lavatories

CROWDS OF VISITORS
More than six million people visited the Great Exhibition. People and carriages literally jammed the streets on cheap "shilling days", and the exhibition made a profit. Prince Albert wanted to encourage "useful knowledge", so the money was used to build new museums, colleges, and the Royal Albert Hall.

VICTORIAN INVENTIONS

The Victorians thought their age was the most exciting, and the Great Exhibition marked a high point of optimism. The Victorians were inventive and practical and loved using the inventions of their age.

1844
MORSE TELEGRAPH
In 1837, English physicists Wheatstone and Cooke patented a telegraph that used letters and a pointer. Seven years later, US inventor, Samuel Morse, sent the first successful telegraph message, using a system of dots and dashes.

1855
PRINTING TELEGRAPH
The printing telegraph, revolutionized communication. In 1839, railways used telegraphs for the first time, and by 1855 news items, and other messages, were being wired around the world.

1873
TYPEWRITER
The first practical typewriter was developed in 1868. Five years later, the first commercial typewriter was produced and soon typewriters began to replace pen and ink in Victorian offices. By 1900, most typists were women.

Exhibits galore

Visitors to the Crystal Palace marvelled at the wealth of exhibits; nothing like this had ever been seen before. The stands were arranged in walk-in galleries, which contained the latest farming and industrial technology. There were even small reproductions of Liverpool docks, and the Coalbrookdale ironworks.

Flags of all nations flew from the roof

The high central vault enclosed two massive elm trees

A cast-iron frame supported 300,000 glass panes

INDUSTRY OF ALL NATIONS
Although more than half the exhibits were British, the Great Exhibition was deliberately planned to be international – to display "the Works of Industry of all Nations". More than 30,000 worldwide exhibitors, took part, and visitors came to London from many countries. A French section attracted much attention, as did a Chinese stand (above).

Industry and art

Prince Albert wanted the Great Exhibition to show that an industrial society could produce beautiful as well as useful goods. The thousands of exhibits were divided into four main categories: raw materials, machinery, manufactured goods, and fine arts. Machinery was the main focus of interest, but the Great Exhibition included an enormous range of arts and crafts, some it highly decorative.

Frontis piece of "The Park and the Crystal Palace"

Ornate French clock

Teasdale's lifeboat

FOOD AND DRINK
Visitors could buy a huge range of food and drink from sandwiches and ices, to teas and coffees. The new Schweppes company provided refreshments, and a steam-powered freezer made ices on the spot.

JEWELS AND MACHINERY
Exhibits ranged from the magnificent Koh-i-nor diamond to a mechanical bed, and James Nasmyth's great steam hammer. Also on show was a printing machine that could print 5,000 copies of *The Illustrated London News* in an hour, and a medal-making machine, which Queen Victoria much admired.

1879
TELEPHONE
Alexander Bell patented the telephone in 1876. Three years later, US inventor Thomas Edison produced this wall-mounted telephone, and London opened its first telephone exchange. By 1900, there were 210,000 telephones in Britain.

1881
ELECTRIC LIGHTING
In 1879 the American Thomas Edison and English inventor Joseph Swan independently invented the light bulb. Electric street lighting appeared in 1881. However, gas lighting remained cheaper, and more popular, until after 1914.

1888
DISC RECORD PLAYER
Edison's phonograph of 1877 showed that sound recording was possible, but US inventor Émile Berliner developed the first disc record player. Within a few years, it began to appear in wealthy Victorian homes.

Working lives

LIFE WAS GRIM FOR working people during the first half of Victoria's reign. The changeover to an industrial society brought them terrible hardship. New types and methods of work were created, and for the first time, massive numbers of people went to work in factories, mills, and foundries (see p. 43). Wages were low, and conditions appalling. Other workers were employed in mines and workshops. New, more specialized occupations appeared, and there was a sharp division between work for women and men. From the 1850s, trade and industry expanded rapidly and working conditions improved.

Men at work

Mechanization destroyed for ever some traditional men's work, such as hand-loom weaving. From the 1850s, new "skilled" occupations appeared such as boiler-making, shipbuilding, and engineering. Men in these industries, together with miners and railway workers, were the so-called "aristocracy of labour". Labourers, dockers, and chain makers, were the "unskilled" workers.

HEALTH AND SAFETY
As there were no laws safeguarding workers' health and safety, factories and foundries were dangerous places. Workers suffered accidents, burns, and disability, and fumes and gases caused new diseases. There were no pensions or benefits, so unemployment meant poverty. People worked for as long as they could.

Ironworkers were skilled workers

The lid was used as a teacup

Sandwich tin filled with bread and dripping (fat)

Workers heated a billycan over a fire to make tea

THE WORKING DAY
Most people today work an eight-hour day. In Victorian Britain, factory machines ran non-stop. Workers, sometimes after a long walk to work, toiled for anything up to 18 hours. From the 1830s, reformers such as Richard Oastler, campaigned to make it illegal to work more than 10 hours a day.

Workers took their own lunch to work

Some employers gave their workers candles

Rules and regulations were strict and usually favoured the employer

RULES & REGULATIONS
FOR ALL
WORKMEN, APPRENTICES, AND BOYS
EMPLOYED ON
THESE PREMISES

All Persons are engaged on condition that they observe the following Rules and Regulations

John Edmunds Printer, Blists Hill

CHILD LABOUR
Thousands of children worked in the mines, factories, and workshops of Victorian Britain – in fact, they made up more than 25 per cent of the labour force. In mines, until 1842, children as young as four years old sat underground in the dark, holding open ventilator doors for coal wagons, pulled by older children. In the mills, little children cleaned under the constantly moving machines. Accidents and deaths were common.

FINES AND WAGES
At work, discipline was harsh. Employers fined workers frequently, even for whistling. Some employers used the hated "truck system", paying workers with goods, or tokens that could only be used at the company store.

Ironworkers repaired tools and carts, and made items from wrought iron

Women at work

Women worked as servants, needleworkers, and in textile mills. Mill workers were the best-paid, and most independent. However, women were paid less than men. Some men opposed women's work, scared that their pay would drop too.

Cookery book

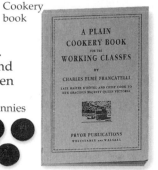

A PLAIN COOKERY BOOK FOR THE WORKING CLASSES
BY CHARLES ELMÉ FRANCATELLI
LATE MAÎTRE D'HÔTEL AND CHIEF COOK TO HER GRACIOUS MAJESTY QUEEN VICTORIA

PRYOR PUBLICATIONS
WHITSTABLE AND WALSALL

Pennies

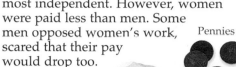

Traditionally, whole families, including women and children, were miners

Seamstresses worked for up to 15 hours a day, sewing by hand

DOUBLE BURDEN

The separation of work and home created a double burden for working women. After a long day, they returned home to clean and care for their families. Some Victorians argued that married women should stay at home, though many could not afford to.

PITBROW LASSIES

The Victorians were horrified by the thought of women miners, because of the dangers, and because they thought it was wrong for men and women to work in such close contact. In 1842, women and children were banned from underground work. Some women, known as "pitbrow lassies" continued working overground until the 1880s, fiercely resisting attempts to end their work.

WEARY AND WORN

Some of the most poorly paid Victorian workers were seamstresses, who worked incredibly long hours, stitching clothes for the rich. Victorian poet, Thomas Hood, described in his poem *Song of the Shirt*, how they sewed "With fingers weary and worn/With eyelids heavy and red...".

Victorian cotton reels

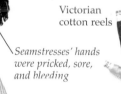

Before sewing machines were invented in 1851, every item of clothing was sewn using a needle and thread

Seamstresses' hands were pricked, sore, and bleeding

FACTORY REFORM

In the early 1800s, many employers believed that shortening hours, or improving conditions, would damage trade and production. Official enquiries revealed terrible working conditions; gradually there were improvements.

1833
Factory Act bans children under 9 from working in factories and mills. No night work for young people under 18.

1842
Mines Commission reveals dreadful conditions. Women, girls, and boys under 10 are banned from underground work.

1844
Factory Act states that 9- to 13-year-olds are to work no more than 6.5 hours a day, and 13- to 18-year-olds and women to work up to 12 hours a day. Dangerous machinery is to be guarded.

1847
'Ten Hours' Act states that women and young people are to work no more than 10 hours a day in factories.

1864-78
A series of acts extends protection from textile mills to other industries.

LIVING CONDITIONS

As industrial towns developed, workers' houses were built quickly and cheaply. Many were cramped back-to-back houses, without running water or bathrooms. Several families lived in one room, and disease was common. Smoke and fumes from nearby factories polluted the atmosphere.

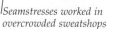

Seamstresses worked in overcrowded sweatshops

Victorian cities

TOWNS AND CITIES GREW rapidly during Victorian times and the population soared (see p. 42). In 1801 only about 33 per cent of the British population lived in towns. By 1901 the figure was 78 per cent. The most spectacular areas of growth were London and the towns and cities of the industrial north, such as Leeds and Manchester. Greater numbers, and the shift of people from country to town in search of work, put much pressure on urban areas. Lack of public amenities and services caused dreadful conditions. From the middle of the century, local authorities introduced improvements.

Street life

Many Victorian cities were seriously overcrowded, and suffered air pollution from factories, or water pollution from open sewers and lack of sanitation. But cities were also bustling centres of activity. Horse-drawn carriages, street sellers, and passers-by, going to banks, shops, or theatres, filled the cities with noise and movement.

Orange seller

STREET TRADERS
A vast army of people earned their living on the streets. Costermongers sold fruit and vegetables from barrows and stalls. Others sold food and drink – pickled whelks, hot eels, ginger beer, lemonade, and hot wine. Children earned pennies by sweeping streets at every crossing.

Ginger beer seller

MARKETS
This painting, *A Busy Market* by Alfred H. Green, shows Victorian people gathered at a market buying a variety of foodstuffs and other goods. Trains brought fresh food from the countryside into towns. Some market traders later became shop owners.

A consumer society

Growing wealth and an outpouring of goods led to a growth of shops and increasing range of consumer items. Manufacturers started to advertise their wares, and department stores appeared. Dickens and Jones, and Harrods in Brompton Road, were among the first. In 1892, Marks and Spencer opened its first shop in Manchester.

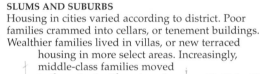

Tin advertising plates

Provision department at Harrods

Display made up of cans of food

SLUMS AND SUBURBS
Housing in cities varied according to district. Poor families crammed into cellars, or tenement buildings. Wealthier families lived in villas, or new terraced housing in more select areas. Increasingly, middle-class families moved to the suburbs (the edge of cities), taking trains or trams into work.

Until the 1860s, many cities were still full of dark courtyards surrounded by lofty wooden houses

Carts, omnibuses, and cabs were pulled by horses

Lines carried trams through the streets

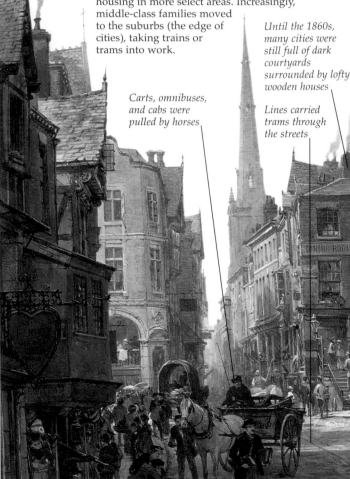

City improvements

Overcrowding, poverty, and lack of sanitation caused frequent outbreaks of fatal diseases such as cholera and typhoid. In 1848, the first Public Health Act was passed, setting up local Boards of Health. Gradually sewers were built, clean water was piped to many homes, and street cleaning and lighting were introduced. From the 1870s, a programme of slum clearance began to pull down some of the worst housing.

The Cross, Eastgate St, Chester by Louise Rayner

Bandstand at Clapham Common, London

Band members wore uniforms

CIVIC PRIDE
From the 1850s, the Victorians took an increasing pride in their cities. Local authorities and businessmen built imposing municipal buildings, such as town halls and libraries, or funded public parks. In every park was a bandstand where, on Sundays, brass bands played popular tunes as Victorian families strolled by. The bands developed from colliery (coal miners') bands and were particularly popular in the north of England.

BOBBIES ON THE BEAT
Crime was a feature of all Victorian cities – from pickpockets to gruesome murderers such as Jack the Ripper. In 1829, Sir Robert Peel had set up a special metropolitan police force in London. Known as "peelers" or "bobbies" the new policemen wore special uniforms and patrolled their areas. By 1856, most towns had a police force.

The production of more varied goods, in the 1860s, gave rise to more shops in the cities

Local authorities introduced street lighting

City of London Fire Brigade equipment

City of London crest

Victorian firefighters used buckets of water to extinguish fires

From the 1860s pavements were improved

Fire-fighting axe with extra-long handle

PUBLIC SERVICES
An effective system of local government was needed to solve city problems. In 1835, the Municipal Corporation Act set up a system of town councils, elected by ratepayers. They could raise money, and were given powers to provide social services such as police, firefighters, lighting, and housing. Two further acts in 1888 and 1894 extended the system.

Angel in the home

FOR THE VICTORIANS THERE was no place like home. The family was central to their lives. As home and work became more and more divided, the home was seen as a refuge from the harsh business world. Taking their lead from the royal family, the middle classes developed an ideal of what family life should be like: peaceful, harmonious, and highly respectable. The woman provided comfort and support; she was the "angel in the home" as one Victorian poet described it. This ideal applied mainly to wealthier families, but later affected everyone. In fact, it still influences family life today.

Home life

Entertainment was an important part of family life. Victorian families spent many hours at home in the drawing room, where they received guests and gathered to play music, read, enjoy games, and talk.

The boxes fit inside each other

Cup and ball game

The aim is to get the ball into the cup, without touching the ball

INDOOR ENTERTAINMENT
In an age before television, the Victorians relied on indoor games for their entertainment. Favourites included card games such as Happy Families, word games, games of skill, and board games such as ludo. Members of the family also read aloud to each other from popular, but respectable, novels.

Journal containing short story

Jigsaw puzzles were attempted by the whole family

Christmas candles

Christmas cards

It became common for families to send Christmas cards to each other

CHRISTMAS CHEER
It was at this time that Christmas became the important family occasion that it is today. Prince Albert introduced the German custom of having a decorated Christmas tree and presents. Thousands of Victorian families enthusiastically followed his example. Christmas cards first appeared in shops in 1846.

Victorian children

Victorian families were often quite large – a single family might consist of as many as six or seven children. Children were treated with strictness by their parents and, at all times, children were expected to be seen, but not heard.

Snakes and ladders board game

Hand-painted mechanical tin toy

NURSERIES
Nannies looked after young children in the nursery. The day consisted of lessons, games, walks, and meals. Obedience was essential. Nurseries were full of toys: dolls, dolls' houses, spinning tops, rocking horses, tin soldiers, and plenty of books.

Victorian homes were heated with coal fires

Women were expected to wear formal dress at home as well as outdoors

Family roles

In wealthy homes the father was head of the family, and his word was never questioned. His role was to go to work and provide for the family. A woman's place was in the home. Until 1882, a married woman's property belonged to her husband. Her role was that of good wife and mother; she was not expected, and often not allowed, to work. From the 1840s, some middle-class women campaigned for greater freedom.

SUNDAY BEST
Going to church and reading the Bible played an important part in Victorian family life. On Sundays, the whole family went to church, and in the evening the father read aloud from the Bible. Popular etiquette (behaviour) books gave advice on how to dress and behave in every situation.

Outside the home gentlemen wore top hats and carried walking sticks

Sheet music

Walking stick

Victorian women carried parasols when outdoors

Home Sweet Home by Walter Dendy Sadler

Embroidery and cross-stitch were considered suitable pastimes for Victorian women

Children dressed in formal clothes, just like adults

MUSICAL EVENINGS
Every Victorian drawing room contained a piano. All young women learned to play, and in the evenings the family gathered round to sing popular, and often sentimental, ballads such as "Home Sweet Home". While women played, men usually sang.

THE LADY CHILD.

PARISIAN 'ARRY
THE COCKNEY ABROAD.

G. W. HUNT.
GEORGE LEYBOURNE.

Life below stairs

MIDDLE-CLASS HOMES WOULD not have survived without servants to do the work. Every upper- and middle-class family, or every family which aspired to be middle class, had servants. Some homes had only a single over-worked maidservant; others employed a whole army, from housekeeper and butler to lowest-paid kitchen maid. Some men went into service as butlers, coachmen, or gardeners, but most servants were women. Life was hard. There was no running hot water, and without washing machines or vacuum cleaners, all housework had to be done by hand.

Household advice

Running a household involved careful organization. The housekeeper or mistress of the house instructed servants, who did the chores. For advice on meals, staff's duties, and cleaning tips, women turned to Mrs Beeton's *Book of Household Management*.

Mrs Beeton's book contains over 1,300 recipes

BEST-SELLER
Isabella Beeton was 21 when she started writing her book. It was full of recipes and tips from how to make a feather bed, to how to deal with childhood illnesses. First published in 1861, her book was the essential home guide. By 1871, it had sold two million copies.

Daily duties

A maid's daily duties included cleaning and lighting the kitchen range, laying tables, emptying slop buckets, scrubbing steps, polishing boots, changing beds, and cleaning the entire house. Maids rose before the family, and rarely went to bed before 10 at night.

Egg whisk

Butter stamp

Jelly mould

Mixing bowl and wooden spoon

COOK
The Victorian middle class ate well. Food included soups, joints of meat, fish, fresh vegetables, and puddings. The cook worked hard all day, preparing meals for the entire household, including servants. Everything had to be made by hand, from bread rolls and soups, to sweet and savoury jellies.

Heavy iron kettle

Handle became red hot when heated

Water was heated on the kitchen range in a kettle, or huge copper pan

SCULLERY MAID
Young girls started in service as soon as they left school. They might begin as scullery or kitchen maids, doing whatever the cook told them to. They worked long hours for little or no pay, sometimes only board and lodging. Eventually, they might become cooks or even housekeepers.

HOUSEHOLD INVENTIONS

New technology led to the development of various domestic appliances. Gradually, they replaced servants, but not until the 20th century. A real innovation was the flushing lavatory. Invented in 1778, it appeared in wealthy homes from the 1850s.

1854
PARAFFIN LAMP
Oil, or paraffin lamps, invented in about 1854, provided a dim light in the drawing room; candles were used in bedrooms. Paraffin spills from the delicate lamps made fire a constant hazard.

1855
CAN OPENER
There were few ways of preserving food other than packing with ice or salting. After the middle of the century, canned foods began to appear: with them came can openers.

1882
ELECTRIC IRON
In 1882, a cordless electric iron was invented. Heat came from an electric element in the stand.

SUITABLE WORK FOR WOMEN

In 1871, over a third of British women aged 12-20 years old were "in service". Some Victorians thought domestic service was more suitable for working-class women than factory work because they learned obedience and household skills. Young women often hated the long hours, constant orders, and lack of freedom.

Cook and kitchen maids at work

Black-lead was actually graphite, a type of carbon

Stove brush

A FILTHY TASK

Open fires warmed the house. A huge iron range in the kitchen provided heat for cooking, and water. Every morning the housemaid swept out the ashes, and brushed, black-leaded, and polished every bit of the range and grates, before laying and lighting coals.

Maids wore starched caps

Kitchen maids bought food fresh each day because there were no refrigerators

White starched apron

Kitchen staff spent most of their waking lives below stairs in the kitchen, scullery, and larder

Low wages

Servants worked from 15 to 18 hours a day, with only half a day off a week. Board and lodging came with the job, but pay was low. According to Mrs Beeton, a junior maid earned £9 to £14 a year; upper servants, such as cooks, between £15 to £25 a year. Conditions varied according to employers.

Food was usually good; the butler was served before the maids

THE SERVANTS' HALL

Wealthy households employed many servants: a housekeeper, cooks, a butler, maids, kitchen boys, gardeners, and perhaps coachmen. Servants were ranked according to importance. Housekeepers, and butlers, for instance, were more important than scullery maids. Servants wore different uniforms according to their job, and followed strict codes of behaviour. They ate together in the kitchen, or servant's hall.

Blue Bag was used in almost every household to make washing whiter

Flat iron

Bar of soap

Wooden pegs

The iron had to be heated on the range

WASHING AND CLEANING

Everything – rooms, ornaments, linen, the family's clothes – had to be spotless. Maids dusted and swept daily. Washing was done by professional laundresses, or in the home by the laundry maid. Soap was grated into tubs filled with warm water, and swirled around with a dolly stick. Washing was rinsed many times, and then aired. Ironing meant using flat irons that had been heated on the range.

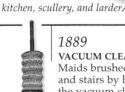

1889
VACUUM CLEANER

Maids brushed carpets and stairs by hand until the vacuum cleaner was invented. Early models, such as this one from 1889, blew dust away rather than sucked it up. In 1901, the first successful suction vacuum cleaner was developed.

1891
ELECTRIC OVEN

Food was cooked on the kitchen range, but by the 1880s, gas cookers were being used. In 1879, an electric oven was developed in which electrically-charged wires heated a pot. By 1891, iron plates incorporated electrical elements.

1891
ELECTRIC KETTLE

The first electric kettle was invented in the US in 1891. It boiled slowly and had non-renewable heating elements fixed in the base. From the 1920s, kettles were made with waterproof elements inside the kettle itself.

Victorian schooling

IN THE EARLY 19TH CENTURY, there were no government-run schools, and no law saying children had to go to school. There were public (fee-paying) schools for the rich, and charity schools for the poor. Few working-class children had any formal education; in fact, some educated people believed that if the poor learned to read and write they would become unhappy with their social position. By the end of Victoria's reign, the government had recognized that working people needed an education, and made all children attend school until they were 13 years old.

Pupils faced the blackboard and copied lessons on to a slate using slate pencils

School funds

Church-run or charity schools provided education for the poor. These schools were free or cost little, but many parents could not afford to let their children stop work to attend. From 1833 the government gave grants to church-run schools, and in 1870 they set up a national system of Board Schools, funded out of local rates (taxes).

Slates were used in schools as they were cheaper than paper

Dinner time at a ragged school

RAGGED SCHOOLS
A strange mixture of schools gave some sort of teaching to poor children. Among them were Sunday Schools, founded in 1780 by English philanthropist Robert Raikes. They spread rapidly, and the Sunday School movement opened weekday schools. Known as "ragged schools", they provided free basic instruction, meals, and clothing for thousands of poor children until Board Schools replaced them.

A white cotton apron kept school clothes clean

Not all parents could afford to buy school boots – some children went barefoot

Pupils sat in rows at metal-framed wooden desks

School subjects

Education for poor children was designed to equip them for work. They learned reading, writing, and arithmetic – the so-called "three Rs". They practised sport, known as drill, and learned about geography and history. Girls were taught how to cook; boys took woodwork lessons.

PUBLIC SCHOOLS
Sons of rich families went to expensive public schools, such as Eton, Rugby, or Westminster (above). Many had been founded in the 15th or 16th centuries. Pupils were taught classical subjects such as Latin and Greek, and educated to become leaders and statesmen. Conditions in public schools were harsh and bullying was common. There were few schools for rich girls, and they were taught mainly by governesses at home. From the 1840s, pioneers such as Emily Davies, Barbara Bodichon, and the Misses Buss and Beale fought for equal rights in girls' education.

RELIGION AND READING
As many schools developed from church-run schools, religion was important. The school day, which lasted from nine to five o'clock, began and ended with prayers. Pupils read from the Bible, and were instructed in its teachings. Poor children were taught obedience, and to accept their station in life.

Children learned about the animal kingdom from this natural history Bible

The properties of geometric shapes were learned by heart

Sphere

Pupils used counting frames, called abacuses, like calculators

Ring

Cone

The ring was used to draw circles

LEARNING BY HEART
All children learned arithmetic, or mathematics. Teachers wrote maths problems on the blackboard, and the children copied them down. The problems were often difficult, and children took tests. The Victorians valued facts more than imagination, and all children learned by heart, chanting aloud their times tables and other facts, over and over again.

EDUCATION REFORMS
As industry developed, the government realized the need to educate working people, and introduced various school reforms. These were mainly for children aged 5 to 13 years old; after that, most working-class children went out to work.

1833
Government provides first ever grant to church schools

1839
Government appoints first school inspectors to check standards

1840
First teachers' training college opens in London

1844
Factory Act states children working in factories must have six half-days' schooling every week

1870
Forster's Education Act sets up nationwide system of Board Schools

1880
Mundella's Education Act makes school compulsory for children aged 5 to 10 years old; leaving age later raised to 13 years

1891
School fees abolished in Board Schools

Teaching practice

Early Victorian teachers were poorly paid, and had little formal training. Sometimes they instructed older pupils, known as monitors, who would then repeat the lesson to the younger class members. From 1839, the government appointed school inspectors to check standards, and test children's progress.

Teachers used canes, or leather straps, to strike naughty pupil's hands, legs, and bottoms

Teacher's bamboo cane

PUNISHMENT
Discipline was strict in Victorian schools. Children who did not learn their lessons had to stand in a corner, wearing a large cone-shaped hat called a dunce's cap. Classes were huge, and talking was forbidden. Teachers were allowed to hit children if they did not behave.

Good attendance medal

GOOD ATTENDANCE
Children often stayed away from school because they had to work, or look after younger children at home. The children who attended regularly received rewards. In 1880, the government made school compulsory for all children aged 5 to 10 years old.

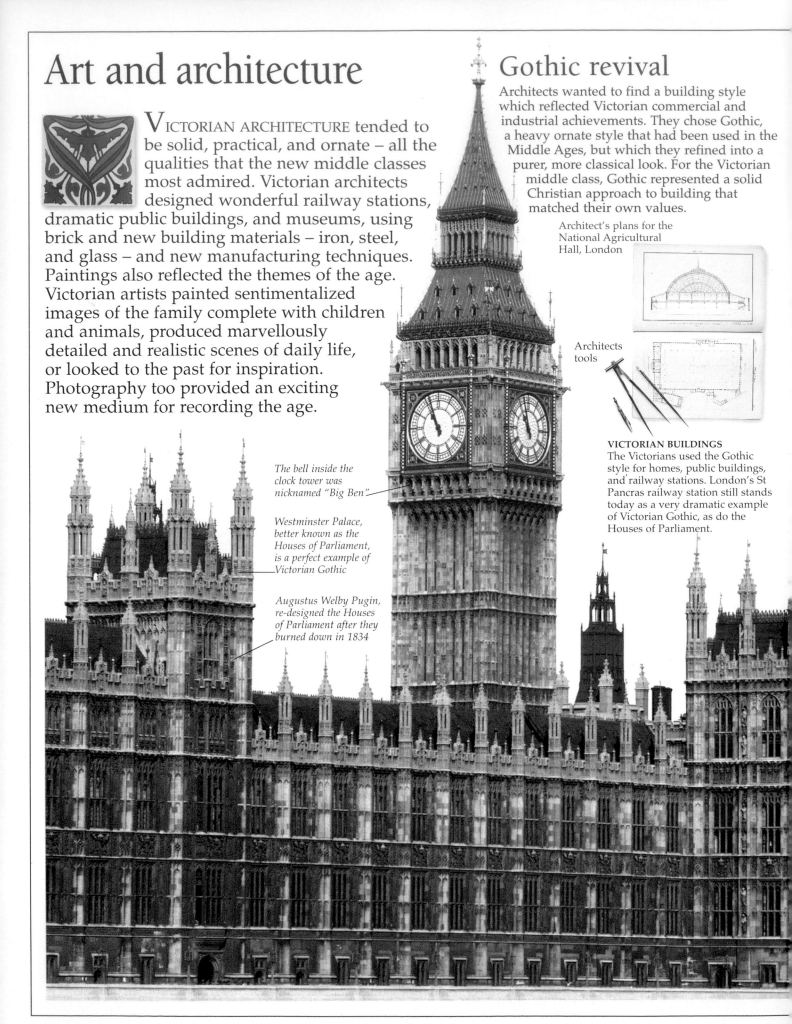

Art and architecture

VICTORIAN ARCHITECTURE tended to be solid, practical, and ornate – all the qualities that the new middle classes most admired. Victorian architects designed wonderful railway stations, dramatic public buildings, and museums, using brick and new building materials – iron, steel, and glass – and new manufacturing techniques. Paintings also reflected the themes of the age. Victorian artists painted sentimentalized images of the family complete with children and animals, produced marvellously detailed and realistic scenes of daily life, or looked to the past for inspiration. Photography too provided an exciting new medium for recording the age.

Gothic revival

Architects wanted to find a building style which reflected Victorian commercial and industrial achievements. They chose Gothic, a heavy ornate style that had been used in the Middle Ages, but which they refined into a purer, more classical look. For the Victorian middle class, Gothic represented a solid Christian approach to building that matched their own values.

Architect's plans for the National Agricultural Hall, London

Architects tools

VICTORIAN BUILDINGS
The Victorians used the Gothic style for homes, public buildings, and railway stations. London's St Pancras railway station still stands today as a very dramatic example of Victorian Gothic, as do the Houses of Parliament.

The bell inside the clock tower was nicknamed "Big Ben".

Westminster Palace, better known as the Houses of Parliament, is a perfect example of Victorian Gothic

Augustus Welby Pugin, re-designed the Houses of Parliament after they burned down in 1834

Visual arts

The Victorian middle classes loved sentimental paintings with titles like *A Hopeless Dawn*, but also colourful paintings of everyday life by William Frith. The age produced fine artists including John Everett Millais, William Holman Hunt, Edward Burne-Jones, and Walter Richard Sickert.

The Lady of Shalott (1888) by J. W. Waterhouse

PRE-RAPHAELITE BROTHERHOOD

In 1848, artists Millais, Hunt, Dante Gabriel Rossetti, influential art critic John Ruskin, and others formed the Pre-Raphaelite Brotherhood. Their distinctive paintings illustrated poetry, moral, religious, and medieval themes. They were full of nature, light, and very romantic.

The subject of this painting is based on an Arthurian legend

ART FOR ALL

Until the 19th century, art had been an aristocratic interest. The nobility had commissioned work for their private collections. Now the Victorians built public art galleries like the one featured in the painting, *The Picture Gallery* by James Hayllar, above. These galleries allowed people of all classes could enjoy works of art.

PHOTOGRAPHY

In the 1830s, pioneer photographer William Fox Talbot developed a successful photographic process. Early cameras were rigid box types, later succeeded by pleated bellows cameras. In the 1880s, the simple box "Brownie" appeared, and amateur photography boomed.

Chemicals and negative

Wet-plate camera

TELLING A STORY

The Victorians liked paintings that told a moral story. The painter, Augustus Egg was very popular. His sombre and graphic paintings showed how unfaithfulness or drunkeness could destroy family life. This helped reinforce Victorian views about the sanctity of marriage, and the woman's role in particular.

Past and present No. 3 Scene of orphaned children since their father died (1858) by Augustus Egg

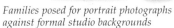

Sepia prints

Families posed for portrait photographs against formal studio backgrounds

ARTS AND CRAFTS MOVEMENT

William Morris

William Morris was a socialist and member of the Pre-Raphaelite Brotherhood. In his writings, and designs, he rejected the ugliness, social injustice, and mass production of industrialism. In 1861, he founded a design firm where both men and women, using traditional techniques and handcrafting, produced wallpaper, furniture, silver work, and fabrics of great simplicity. Morris believed that people should be surrounded by things that combined beauty and usefulness. The style was known as Arts and Crafts, and was very influential.

Morris-style ceramic tile

William Morris wallpaper

Ironically, Morris's designs were so popular they were copied and mass produced

William Morris's designs are still popular today

A new reading public

THE VICTORIANS LOVED reading – novels, books on self improvement, newspapers, magazines, "penny-dreadfuls" (sensational magazines), popular histories, travel guides, and even comics. Without cinema or television, books were a real source of pleasure. Greater educational opportunities increased the demand for books and steam printing, introduced in 1814, lowered the costs of production. Trains distributed books and periodicals all over the country. Railway bookstalls, owned by W. H. Smith, and a growing number of libraries meant that books were more widely available. The reading public, and the market for books, had never been bigger.

A literate nation

Some people argue that literacy increased in the 19th century. But self-improvement was an important part of working-class culture and most people could read and write. Adults without a formal education taught themselves through local mechanics' institutes and other associations.

PUBLIC LIBRARIES
Access to libraries was originally limited to the wealthy. Even London's British Museum, and Chetham Library in Manchester, which were free, closed before working-class people finished work. Workers clubbed together to buy books; sometimes industrialists and philanthropists provided libraries. In 1850, the Public Libraries Act enabled towns to use rates to build free public libraries for all.

Charles Dickens

The most popular Victorian novelist was Charles Dickens. His first novel, *Pickwick Papers* (1837), was a success and was followed by *Oliver Twist* (1839), and many others. As a child Dickens had known poverty. He wrote with compassion, and humour, about social injustices.

Illustrated instalment of Dickens' *Oliver Twist*

MONTHLY EPISODES
Dickens' novels were serialized in magazines, in monthly episodes, before being published in book form. As a writer, Dickens was a master of suspense; each episode left his public waiting eagerly for the next installment. He also gave public readings to packed audiences in Britain and the United States.

Charles Dickens at his writing desk

Dickens is using a quill pen – a feather made into a pen

Dickens created wonderful characters – Mr Micawber, Sarey Gamp, Fagin, Bill Sykes and Nancy – who are still enjoyed today

Charlotte
Brontë

Books for all

The Victorian age produced some of the finest novels in the English language. There was something for every taste, from Mrs Gaskell's *Mary Barton* (1848), a moving story of life in the industrial north, to the Gothic horrors of Bram Stoker's *Dracula* (1897), and the great novels of George Eliot, or Mary Ann Evans as she was really named. The Victorians also enjoyed highly sentimental verse, as well as books about history and travel.

Daily papers

Sherlock Holmes is one of fiction's greatest sleuths

Illustration from *Tess of the d'Urbervilles*

"TESS OF THE D'URBERVILLES"
By THOMAS HARDY

BRONTE SISTERS
Charlotte, Anne, and Emily Brontë were born in Yorkshire. They wrote romantic novels. Charlotte is best-known for *Jane Eyre* (1847); Emily for the dramatic *Wuthering Heights* (1847); and Anne for *The Tenant of Wildfell Hall* (1848). In order to be published the sisters wrote under men's names.

THOMAS HARDY
Hardy set his work against the background of a disappearing English countryside. His early novels such as *Far from the Madding Crowd* (1874) were very popular. But Victorians were shocked by *Tess of the d'Urbervilles* (1891) and *Jude the Obscure* (1895) because they described human relationships too realistically.

A POPULAR PRESS
The Times dated back to 1785, but it was expensive and catered for the upper classes. Newspapers were taxed, and there were harsh laws about content. In 1855, after a long battle for press freedom, the tax was removed, and newspapers suddenly became cheaper. They rolled non-stop off the new printing presses, and soon everyone was reading a paper from *The Daily Telegraph*, the first of the penny papers, through to the more sensational *Daily Mail*. After 1850, children's comics also appeared, featuring cartoons and heroic adventures.

DETECTIVE FICTION
As police became part of daily life, detective novels appeared. In 1868, Willkie Collins published *The Moonstone*, featuring Sergeant Cuff, the first detective hero in English fiction. In the 1890s, Arthur Conan Doyle thrilled audiences with *The Adventures of Sherlock Holmes* (1892).

Alice

Alice grows taller after drinking from a bottle

We can learn a lot about Victorian daily life from Dickens' writings

Books for children

Victorian children could bury their noses in a growing number of books written just for them. Some were stories; some provided examples of how boys and girls should behave; others such as Edward Lear's nonsense verse were sheer entertainment. Favourites included Robert Louis Stephenson's *Treasure Island* (1883), the two *Jungle Books* (1894, 1895) by Rudyard Kipling, and *Black Beauty* (1877) by Anna Sewell.

LEWIS CARROL
The first real fantasy tale for children was *Alice's Adventures in Wonderland* (1865). It was written by Lewis Carrol, whose real name was Charles Dodgson, for a friend's daughters. Completely free of any moralizing, Alice's adventures fascinated Victorian children.

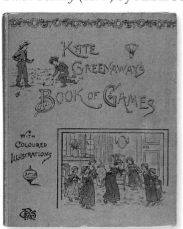

Drawing by Kate Greenaway

Dickens' novel David Copperfield (1850) was based on his own early life

WORDS AND PICTURES
During the 1860s, children's picture books appeared in every middle-class nursery. Kate Greenaway produced beautiful illustrations, which appeared in everything from alphabet books to collections of her own verses. Most of them featured children.

Social reform

Victorian society was far from equal. Industrialization created a wealthy middle class based on trade and industry. It also created a huge labouring or working class, much of which lived in terrible conditions. Poverty and human suffering were widespread. Official reports regularly investigated social problems, but solutions were not easy. Some wealthy Victorians believed in a philosophy of *laissez faire*, or "let it be", and thought governments should not intervene. But public concern grew, and major social reforms were introduced.

Blowing the whistle

In the 1840s, observers such as Friedrich Engels, and Henry Mayhew, described dreadful working-class living conditions in Manchester and London. In the 1890s, reformers Charles Booth and Seebohm Rowntree estimated that at least 20 per cent of the population did not have enough to live on.

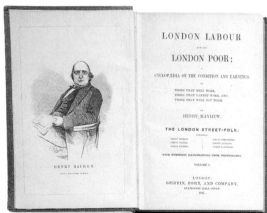

SURVEY ON THE VERY POOR
In *London Labour and the London Poor* (1851–62), Henry Mayhew wrote about the poor using their own words. It described the lives of the poor, from "toshers" who scraped a living from refuse, to desperate seamstresses, who worked as prostitutes when sewing was scarce.

MEDICINE AND HEALTH

In 1842, Edwin Chadwick's official report showed that more than 50 per cent of towns in Britain had impure water supplies. Cholera epidemics killed thousands. Gradually, the Victorians understood that dirt and disease were linked and introduced medical and public health reforms.

Private philanthropy

The plight of the poor haunted the Victorian middle classes. Private or church-funded charity came before government help. Individuals, known as philanthropists, spent their lives helping poor people, raising money, setting up soup kitchens and hostels, and publicizing the problems. Often religious beliefs inspired their work.

A RELIGIOUS ARMY
In 1865, a Methodist minister, William Booth, horrified by poverty in London's East End, founded what later became known as the Salvation Army. A religious organization, run on military lines, it provided shelter, clothes, and food for the destitute.

Salvation Army bonnet

Social workers

Many middle-class women became involved in good works; in some ways they were forerunners of today's social workers. Sometimes poor people distrusted both them and male philanthropists.

Mrs Fry reading to the prisoners in Newgate Prison

1846
ETHER INHALER
Originally, operations took place without painkillers. In 1846, an American dentist used ether to make his patients unconscious; soon surgeons began to use the new anaesthetic.

1855
STETHOSCOPE
In 1819, French doctor René Laennec had inve[n]ted a tube for listening to a patient's heartbeat. By 1[855?] it had developed into a stethoscope, similar to those which doctors us[e] today for listening to heart and lungs.

MODEL HOUSING

Many rich people tried to deal with the problems of slum housing and homelessness. Octavia Hill bought and converted slum properties. In 1866 American banker George Peabody gave £100,000 to provide "new model dwellings" with gardens for London's poor. Dr Barnado founded homes for destitute children. Ultimately, the problems were too great for individuals to solve by themselves.

Peabody Square, Westminster

Peabody's houses were light and airy

Women prisoners took their children into prison so that they would not end up on the streets

ELIZABETH FRY

Elizabeth Fry, a Quaker, tirelessly took up the cause of prison reform. Shocked by the filthy and disgusting conditions she found in Newgate Prison, London, she formed an association to help women prisoners. The association found the women work and educated their children.

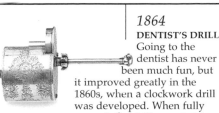

Public reforms

The Victorian middle class believed in self-help, but eventually governments had to take action. In Parliament, Lord Shaftesbury led the fight for factory legislation. In 1875, a major public health act was passed; other laws improved working conditions, and housing.

Lord Shaftesbury campaigned for factory acts, set up "ragged schools" and championed the cause of young chimney sweeps

CLIMBING BOYS

The horrors of child labour caused public outcry. Some young boys worked as chimney sweeps in wealthy houses, climbing up chimneys to remove soot. Many died from suffocation or severe burns. Charles Kingsley's novel, *The Water Babies* (1863), publicized their suffering.

Chimney sweep's brush

Most people in workhouses were unemployed or elderly

WORKHOUSES

Some people believed the poor caused their own difficulties by not working hard enough. Those who could not support themselves, were forced to enter workhouses where conditions were deliberately harsh. Families were separated, food was bad, and work was meaningless. Slowly, governments saw the need for proper help; the first state pensions and benefits came in 1908.

1864
DENTIST'S DRILL
Going to the dentist has never been much fun, but it improved greatly in the 1860s, when a clockwork drill was developed. When fully wound, the drill operated for up to two minutes at a time.

1867
ANTISEPTIC SPRAY
In the 1850s, French chemist, Louis Pasteur, finally proved that bacteria, or germs, caused disease. In 1867, English surgeon, Joseph Lister, used a carbolic spray as an antiseptic, spraying it on wounds and instruments to kill bacteria.

1880

ENDOSCOPE
During the 19th century, Victorian doctors developed instruments known as endoscopes, for looking inside the body without cutting it open. This one dates from 1880.

Fight for rights

WORKING PEOPLE HAD no rights at the beginning of the Victorian period, and no say in government. Middle-class employers saw the new industrial workers as "hands" to be owned and used. But as the century wore on, the industrial working class, who sold their time and skills in exchange for wages, recognized their own importance to Victorian society, and began to fight back against hardship and exploitation. Through protest movements, trade unions, and other organizations, the working class demanded their right to better conditions, and a political voice. It was a long struggle, but by 1901 much had been achieved.

Parliament

Political power rested with Parliament. It consisted of an entirely unelected, hereditary House of Lords and an elected House of Commons. Until the 1830s, elections were corrupt and members of parliament represented the landowners rather than the commercial middle class or working class. Pressure from both classes forced huge changes.

House of Commons

CHARTISM
In 1838 a huge mass movement – Chartism – emerged. A People's Charter was presented to Parliament demanding the right to vote, secret ballots, an end to the law that stated MPs had to be landowners, and other reforms. Thousands of people demonstrated in support, but Parliament rejected all demands. Chartism died in 1848, but most of its demands later became law.

TRADE UNIONS
After Chartism, workers turned to trade unions to represent their interests at work. The struggle for their right to form unions was a bitter one. In the 1850s, highly skilled workers – miners, railway workers, and engineers – formed powerful unions that could negotiate with employers who needed their labour. In the late 1880s, militant workers such as dockers and the match girls improved their conditions through strikes.

Acts of 1871 and 1875 legalized trade unions

POLITICAL PARTIES

Today's political parties were formed during the Victorian period. The Conservative Party emerged in the 1830s from the old Tories. Its first prime minister was Sir Robert Peel. The Liberal Party emerged in the late 1850s from a mix of Whigs and radicals. Both parties competed for government. After 1867 they introduced much-needed social reforms to win the working-class vote. In 1893 socialist Kier Hardie founded the Independent Labour Party (ILP). By 1900 it had evolved into the Labour Party.

A meeting of the Women's Co-operative Guild, held at Burton-on-Trent

Interior of the House of Commons (1858) by Joseph Nash

CAMPAIGNING WOMEN

Women were active in all political pressure groups. They campaigned in the Chartist movement – an early demand was votes for both men and women – and formed their own trade unions. Middle-class women, such as Josephine Butler and Emily Davies, fought strongly for the rights of women. In 1883, married working-class women found a powerful political voice when they formed the Women's Co-operative Guild. Through the Guild they campaigned successfully for maternity and other rights.

Voting card

A NEW ELECTORATE

In 1832, middle-class men had won the vote after an aggressive campaign that used working-class support. Reform of Parliament began almost immediately, but the working class, still without the vote, felt bitter. They continued to agitate, and in 1867 and 1884 the vote was extended to many working-class men.

After 1832, industrial towns such as Manchester and Sheffield could send MPs to Parliament

There were no women MPs until 1918

Before 1832, only landowners could be Members of Parliament (MPs)

Between 1832 and 1901, the House of Commons became more representative of the population

HOME RULE IN IRELAND

Ireland was a major political issue throughout the Victorian period. Poverty, land shortage, and a dreadful famine in 1845–48 brought terrible hardship to the majority Catholic population. Irish nationalism grew, and by the 1870s groups such as the Fenians were demanding Home Rule, or self-government for Ireland. In 1886 and again in 1893, Liberal Prime Minister William Gladstone introduced Home Rule Bills to Parliament, but both failed.

REFORM ACTS

In 1832 some 435,000 people had the vote. By 1885 the number had risen to 5.6 million. Women were completely excluded. It was not until 1918, after years of fierce campaigning, that women finally won the vote.

1832
First Reform Act gives the vote to middle-class men; also creates new electoral districts in industrial regions.

1858
Property qualification for MPs is abolished; non-landowners can stand for Parliament.

1867
Second Reform Act gives the vote to most urban working-class men.

1872
Ballot Act: voters can cast votes in secret.

1884
Third Reform Act extends the vote to most rural working-class men.

Highdays and holidays

LIFE IMPROVED FOR most people during the second half of Queen Victoria's reign. Working hours shortened, wages rose steadily, and prices of goods and food fell. From 1850, factories closed on Saturday afternoons and, in 1871, a new law introduced four official bank holidays a year. For the first time since the upheavals of the Industrial Revolution, and particularly from the 1880s onwards, most working people had more money and free time for entertainment. The more leisured middle class also took up various new pastimes. Theatre, music, opera, sport, and travel flourished. With money to spend, and time to spare, the Victorians created what was effectively the start of a leisure industry.

Thomas Cook poster advertising holidays abroad

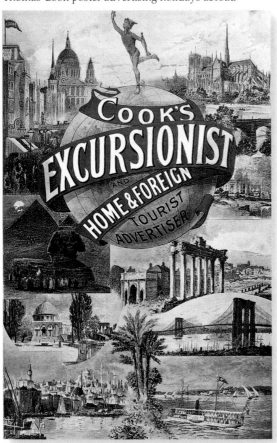

COOK'S TOURS
In 1841, Thomas Cook started a travel firm and, in 1851, made handsome profits running excursion trains to the Great Exhibition. By the 1880s, with the rise of steamships and continental railways, Cook's firm was guiding middle-class tourists around Europe, the Holy Land (Palestine), and the Egyptian pyramids.

Seaside trips

Railways and cheap fares made seaside holidays possible. Increasingly the Victorians made day trips to the sea or, if they could afford it, stayed for a week or more. Blackpool was the first seaside town dedicated entirely to the holiday trade; others included Scarborough, Southport, Lytham, Broadstairs, and resorts in Kent and Sussex.

Punch and Judy puppets

Punch and Judy shows were performed in tents on the beach

BEACH LIFE
Beaches were a hive of activity, with donkey rides and Punch and Judy shows. The Victorians built great metal piers where pierrot (clown) shows and brass bands provided entertainment. Swimming was popular, but, because of Victorian morality, costumes had to cover most of the body.

As resorts grew, guest houses and smart hotels sprang up

On the Promenade, Brighton by Theodore Hines

Ladies carried parasols to protect their heads from the heat of the sun

Men and women strolled along the promenade dressed in their Sunday best

Even on the hottest days, men, women, and children remained covered up

Promenades were built so that visitors could breathe in the sea air without having to walk on the sand

Dogs scavenged near the beach for scraps of food

Music concerts

In 1871, the Royal Albert Hall opened in London. For the first time, middle-class audiences flocked to public concert halls to hear music by the composers Mendelssohn and Verdi, or light opera such as *The Pirates of Penzance* by Gilbert and Sullivan. Theatre-going was also popular.

Musical programme

MUSIC HALLS

Working-class music lovers went to music halls, or played in brass bands. By 1880, there were more than 500 music halls in Britain. For a few pennies, audiences could enjoy comic turns, or sing along to popular, sometimes rude, songs.

PUBLIC HOUSES

Some middle-class Victorians worried about drunkenness among working people. But pubs were lively places, where working people could relax with friends and play games such as dominoes and cards.

Dominoes

Playing cards

THEATRE ROYAL.
Mr. J. L. TOOLE
AS THE "ARTFUL DODGER" IN OLIVER TWIST.

London theatre poster

Sport for all

Sport became a national pastime. Cricket, rugby, and golf were all popular and sportsmen, such as the cricketer W. G. Grace, became national heroes. Lawn tennis began in 1874; the first Wimbledon men's championships were held in 1877.

Leather football and rugby ball

PROFESSIONAL FOOTBALL

In 1848, the Football Association established national rules, and the game began to be the national obsession it is today. Different areas formed clubs, and fans travelled, by bus, tram, and train to support "their" team.

Wooden tennis racket

CYCLING FUN

From 1884, when the "safety" bicycle appeared, cycling became a favourite pursuit. By 1901, there were more than 2,000 cycling clubs in Britain. Cycling was cheap, and brought a new freedom.

Safety bicycle

Air-filled rubber tyres gave a soft, smooth ride

Lemonade bottle

Beer bottles

Gas lights illuminated the promenade

All piers had a wooden and metal bandstand, surrounded by chairs

Men and women swam separately

The Victorians went into the sea from special bathing huts

Empire-builders

WHEN QUEEN VICTORIA came to the throne, Britain already governed parts of India, Canada, and Australia, and had various other overseas colonies. Together they formed the British Empire. Britain had been gaining overseas influence and possessions steadily since the 1600s, but until Victorian times, the Empire had grown slowly. But from the 1870s, in a search for new trade markets, and facing competition from other nations such as Germany and France, Britain set out to win new territories and influence, particularly in Africa. By 1901 empire-building was virtually over. Queen Victoria ruled over nearly one-quarter of the world's people. The British Empire was the largest the world had ever seen.

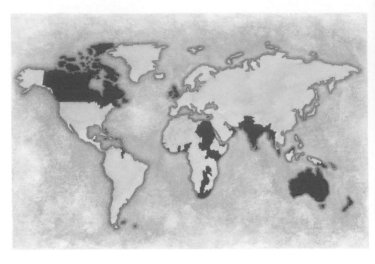

TRADING EMPIRE
The British Empire spread over every continent of the world. Its territories, shown in red, included self-governing dominions such as Australia and Canada, and strategic islands such as Singapore and Hong Kong. The Empire was built on trade. Britain imported raw materials such as cotton, tea, and rubber, from the Empire and exported manufactured goods, from locomotives to machine tools, back to the colonies.

Jewel in the crown

For the Victorians, India symbolized the Empire. Its resources, exotic peoples and regions, and long-standing connection with Britain made it special – "the jewel in the crown" as Queen Victoria said. British involvement grew from trading stations set up by the East India Company in 1600. By 1900, Britain ruled virtually the entire subcontinent. An Anglo-Indian army, and huge civil service of British and Indian officials governed the vast region.

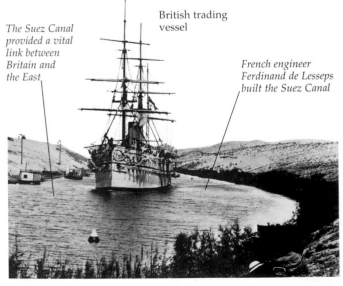

The Suez Canal provided a vital link between Britain and the East

British trading vessel

French engineer Ferdinand de Lesseps built the Suez Canal

EAST OF SUEZ
In 1869, the Suez Canal opened, linking the Mediterranean Sea and the Indian Ocean. Six years later, British Prime Minister Benjamin Disraeli, a keen supporter of the Empire, bought the controlling interest in the canal from the Khedive (Viceroy) of Egypt. British control of the Suez Canal shortened the route to India, gave increased access to the East, and, from 1882, gave Britain effective rule over Egypt.

Battle of Sepoys, India, 1857

Three regiments of sepoys mutinied

Scramble for Africa

In the 1870s much of Africa remained free of European control. However, a "scramble for Africa" began, and by 1900, Britain, competing against other empire-builders, such as France and Germany, gained most: Kenya, Uganda, Nigeria, and southern Africa, including Rhodesia (Zimbabwe).

INDIAN MUTINY

British expansion and lack of respect for religious or local customs often led to conflict. In 1857, Indian soldiers, known as sepoys, rebelled against British army officers. Rebellion led to terrible bloodshed. Following the rebellion, the British aimed to rule with greater sensitivity, but saw India as a permanent part of the Empire. An independence movement emerged, and in 1885, the Indian National Congress met for the first time.

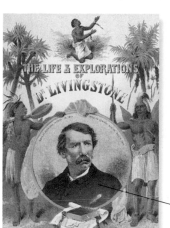

MISSIONARIES

Middle-class Victorians had a strong sense of duty. Rudyard Kipling wrote with feeling about the "white man's duty" to the peoples of the Empire. Missionaries travelled through Africa and Asia preaching Christianity, but also setting up schools and hospitals. David Livingstone was a Scottish traveller and missionary. He spent 30 years in Africa, exploring the Zambezi region, and working with local people. His travels inspired Victorians.

David Livingstone

Livingstone's compass and magnifying glass

Christmas in India (1881) by E. K. Johnson

India offered important career opportunities for middle-class British administrators and traders

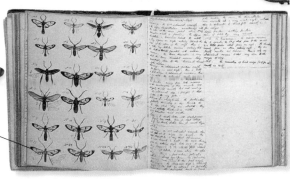

Naturalists drew these insects in the Amazon region of South America

EXPLORATION

British explorers travelled enthusiastically through countries hardly known by Europeans. John Speke and Samuel Baker explored the source of the Nile. Mary Kingsley travelled through Angola. They sent back specimens and accounts which were housed in new institutions such as the Royal Geographic Society.

Some Indians worked as house servants to the British

Many Indians feared the British would force them to become Christians

LEAVING HOME

This painting *The Last of England* (1860) by Ford Madox Brown shows a couple leaving Britain. From the 1850s, thousands of Britons emigrated to the colonies in search of a better life, most particularly Australia, Canada, and New Zealand. Many were Irish, fleeing from terrible famine and poverty in their own country.

The British set up tea plantations in India and Ceylon

Victorians at war

WITH ITS STRONG NAVY and economic supremacy, Britain faced no serious threats until the late 19th century. Compared with the global conflicts to come, Britain was not involved in major wars, apart from the Crimean War whose horrors shocked the British public. British foreign policy, particularly under Lord Palmerston, aimed to defend, and expand, Britain's interests. British troops were constantly in action, either policing the Empire, or putting down rebellions. They fought Maoris in New Zealand, Jamaicans in the Caribbean, and brutally crushed the Indian Mutiny. In Africa, defeats by the Sudanese at Khartoum in 1885, and the Zulus in 1879 caused a surge of intense patriotism. By 1899, Britain was engaged in a bitter conflict in South Africa, known as the Boer War.

Crimean War

The Crimean War was fought to prevent Russian expansion into Turkish-controlled lands. In 1854 British, French, Turkish, and Sardinian forces arrived in the Crimea, next to the Black Sea, to attack the Russian fortress of Sevastapol. The war ended in 1856 with the Russian defeated.

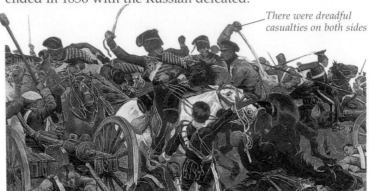

There were dreadful casualties on both sides

THE SIEGE OF SEBASTAPOL
The allies defeated Russian forces at Alma, then laid siege to Sebastapol. It dragged on for nearly a year, through a desperately cold winter. At the battles of Balaclava, and Inkerman (above) the allies defeated Russian attempts to break the siege. Newspaper reports fuelled public outrage at the length, horrors, and mismanagement of the war.

Boer War

In 1899, war broke out in South Africa between Dutch settlers, known as Boers, and Britain, for control of the mineral-rich republics of Transvaal and the Orange Free State. Initially the Boers were successful, defeating the British at Mafeking, Kimberley, and Ladysmith. With much flag-waving and public enthusiasm, Britain sent huge reinforcements. They recaptured Mafeking, and the Boers were finally defeated. In 1902, the republics were absorbed into the British Empire.

British troops at Kimberley

British troops in action during the Boer War

Breech-loading, long-barrelled rifles were introduced in the 1870s

MILITARY TECHNOLOGY
Victorian armies depended on horses to carry supplies, and soldiers. Bayonets remained common, but there were some important, and deadly, technological developments. Breech-loading weapons, smokeless powder, and rapid-firing machine guns all transformed warfare. The use of breech-loading rifles such as the Martini-Henri gave British soldiers a huge advantage over indigenous peoples.

New firearms were loaded from behind the barrel rather than in front

New developments in telegraphy, and photography in the Victorian period brought home the realities of war for the first time

A MISMANAGED WAR

The Crimean War was bungled. The British army suffered from lack of preparation, conflicting orders, and shortage of supplies. At the battle of Balaclava during one particular attack, confused orders sent the British cavalry on an heroic, but suicidal charge against massed Russian artillery. Nearly half the cavalry were killed or wounded. Tennyson's poem, *The Charge of the Light Brigade* (1852), immortalized the disaster.

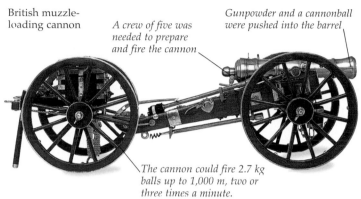

British muzzle-loading cannon

A crew of five was needed to prepare and fire the cannon

Gunpowder and a cannonball were pushed into the barrel

The cannon could fire 2.7 kg balls up to 1,000 m, two or three times a minute.

ROYAL NAVY

The Victorians were proud of their navy, which was the largest and most powerful in the world. Industrial developments transformed naval warfare; by the 1880s, steam-driven ironclads (wooden warships with armour plating) and steamships were replacing wood and sail. Uniforms were introduced and naval service became a prestigious career. The practice of sending British "gunboats" to trouble spots led to the rise of "jingoism" – an extreme form of nationalism – which took its name from a popular music hall song.

TOMMIES

Khakis were a dull yellowish-brown colour

By the 1890s, the ordinary British soldier had acquired a new importance, and a nickname: Tommy Atkins. British soldiers also had a new uniform – khaki. First worn in India, it took its name from the Hindustani word for "dust", and provided better camouflage than the red coats worn previously.

Victoria Cross

Queen Victoria instituted the medal in 1856

Victoria Cross medals are made out of bronze from Russian cannons captured during the Crimean War

SOLDIERS OF THE QUEEN

The horrors of the Crimea focused British public opinion on the ordinary soldier. Britain's standing army was quite small, and ordinary soldiers were treated badly. From the 1860s, reforms were introduced and brutal practices, such as flogging, were outlawed. Queen Victoria took a particular interest in the army, and "her" ordinary soldiers. She personally awarded medals to soldiers of all ranks, and following her wishes, the Victoria Cross was created for outstanding bravery.

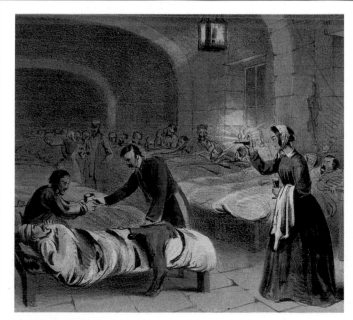

FIELD HOSPITALS

More soldiers died of disease and infection in the Crimea than their wounds. Field medicine was primitive, amputations took place without anaesthetic, and cleanliness and medical supplies were almost unknown. In 1855, Florence Nightingale arrived in Scutari with a handful of women nurses. Despite opposition, she demanded supplies, introduced sanitation, and created the first effective military hospital. In doing so, she revolutionized nursing, and made it an acceptable profession for women.

The Victorian legacy

IN 1901, QUEEN VICTORIA died, and the Victorian period came to an end. It had been a time of extraordinary change. Any adult alive in 1837 would have hardly recognized the Britain of 1901. Great industrial towns and cities had emerged, trains ran through the countryside trailing long streamers of smoke, steamships stood in the docks, massive bridges and tunnels were monuments to Victorian engineering. Most people were better fed, clothed, healthier, and more educated. Cities were full of shops, which contained previously unimaginable goods, made in British factories, or imported from Britain's worldwide empire.

End of an era

The Victorians' energy and innovation made them world leaders. But in 1901, Britain was no longer the world's leading power. Since the 1870s, the United States and Germany had industrialized, and were rapidly overtaking Britain. Poverty was still widespread, Britain was at war, and there were problems in the British Empire. For some Victorians, the future looked less optimistic than the past.

Period of change

The Victorians transformed Britain from an agricultural country to a world industrial power, and in the process achieved an extraordinary amount, particularly in terms of industry, engineering, science, public health, and education. Victorian technology, empire-building, and ways of thinking, also influenced the rest of the world, sometimes with damaging effects.

LASTING MONUMENTS
Victorians built things to last, and Britain today is full of reminders: statues, railway stations, bridges, public libraries, school buildings, even seaside piers. From family life to foreign travel, the Victorian influence on daily life was enormous. And its impact did not stop in the 19th century. Much of what we have today – from trains, telephones, light bulbs, and cameras, to sports, and modern medicine – came from the Victorians.

The Queen Victoria Memorial stands in front of Buckingham Palace, London

DEATH OF A QUEEN
In 1897 Britain celebrated Queen Victoria's Diamond Jubilee – 60 years on the throne. European heads of state and rulers from all parts of the Empire came to London to join the celebrations. Just over three years later, Victoria died aged 81. Her coffin was carried on a gun carriage through London. Thousands of mourners from Britain and the Empire lined the streets to watch it pass.

Penny Black

POSTAL SERVICE
Victorians not only developed trains, buses, and trams, but also our postal service. In 1840, Rowland Hill decided that anyone sending a letter should pay in advance, and introduced the first postage stamp. Bearing an image of the queen, the first stamp cost one old penny, and was known as a "Penny Black".

The Victoria and Albert Museum, London, started in 1899

The museum houses art and culture from around the world

Charles Darwin

SHOCKS AND CHALLENGES
Despite the changes around them, most Victorians believed in an unchanging social order. They were God-fearing people, and Christianity was important. Many took the Bible quite literally. In 1859, Charles Darwin published *The Origin of Species*, suggesting that all life forms might have evolved over millions of years, and that humans might be descended from apes. His views shocked the Victorians.

Darwin's ideas remained controversial until the 20th century

EDUCATION FOR ALL
The fact that any British child can have a free education is very much due to the Victorians. Before the 19th century, learning of all kinds was restricted to a small and privileged minority. After some reservations, the Victorians recognized that an industrial population needed access to learning, and to culture. They built not only schools but also museums, libraries, and art galleries that are still with us today.

In the 1890s, three out of every four ships in the world were built in British shipyards

Co-op department store, circa 1900

CO-OPERATION, NOT COMPETITION
Not all Victorians accepted industrial society. Some early socialists such as Robert Owen sought to build a new society based on co-operation rather than competition. Today the Co-op is the most visible reminder of the co-operative movement. First set up in the 1840s, Co-op shops aimed to provide food and other goods at prices that working people could afford.

WORLD IMPACT
During Victorian times the world became more accessible. World trade, improved transport, and better communications meant that once-distant places, unusual foods, and even foreign words, increasingly became part of daily life.

Bolton Wanderers Football Club (1881)

PRIDE AND PATRIOTISM
Many Victorians – although not all – were confident, and idealistic about their achievements. They believed the Empire would last for ever, and the progress they had made in so many fields – education, industry, engineering, medicine, even sport – would eventually benefit everyone. They were proud of their achievements, and of Britain. Pride and idealism were reflected in popular literature and songs, which emphasized determination, fair play, and the superiority of British values.

Team sports are a popular legacy from the Victorian period

As today, the Victorians believed that sport encouraged health, competitiveness, and team spirit

Important dates

1837	Victoria comes to the throne
1840	Marriage of Queen Victoria and Prince Albert
1840s	Railway "mania" hits Britain
1842	Mines Act bans women and children from underground work in mines
1844	Factory Act prevents children under nine years old from working in factories
1845–8	Potato famine in Ireland: nearly a million die and thousands emigrate
1848	Public Health Act sets up board of health with powers to improve sanitation in towns; other acts follow 1872, 1875
1851	Great Exhibition held in London; marks high-point of Victorian trade, which grows steadily until 1870s
1851	Amalgamated Society of Engineers, the engineering union, founded
1854–6	Crimean War in Russia; 4,600 soldiers die in battle; 13,000 are wounded; 17,500 die of disease
1861	Prince Albert dies from typhoid
1869	John Sainsbury opens a small grocery shop in London; it later develops into a nationwide chain of shops
1874	Jesse Boot begins to sell herbal medicines in Nottingham; by 1900 there are 160 Boots shops countrywide
1870	Forster's Education Act makes primary education available for all
1870s	Cheap, imported foodstuffs transform daily diet
1875	Artisans Dwelling Act enables local authorities to pull down and replace slum dwellings
1881	First electric street lighting appears
1882	Married Women's Property Act enables married women to have legal ownership over their property
1890	Electric trains run on London's underground railway
1891	Primary education in state schools becomes free
1895	Herbert Austin opens motor car factory in Birmingham
1899–1902	Boer War in South Africa
1901	Queen Victoria dies aged 81

Victorian facts and figures

THE VICTORIAN AGE LASTED from 1837 to 1901, exactly the period of Queen Victoria's reign. It was a time of immense change. The population soared, towns and cities increased in size, transport and work were completely transformed. These pages provide some useful facts and figures, including key dates, and a list of places where you can discover more about this fascinating period of history.

Population in Great Britain in millions

1901

1851

21   37

THE ROYAL FAMILY TREE
Queen Victoria came to the throne almost by accident. Both her uncles, George IV and William IV, left no surviving heirs, although they both had a number of illegitimate children. This meant that when William IV died in 1837, the throne passed to Victoria, the daughter of his younger brother, the Duke of Kent, who had died in 1820. Victoria married her cousin Albert. They had nine children. Their eldest son, "Bertie", succeeded Victoria as Edward VII. His great-granddaughter is Elizabeth II, the present queen.

THE ROYAL FAMILY TREE
Queen Victoria came to the throne almost by accident. Her grandfather was George III. He had 15 children, but none of them, except his fourth son, the Duke of Kent, Victoria's father, left legitimate heirs. After George III's death in 1820, his eldest son succeeded him as George IV. He died in 1830, and his brother succeeded him as William IV. When William died in 1837, Victoria was the only choice. Victoria married her cousin Albert. They had nine children. Their eldest son, "Bertie", succeeded Victoria as Edward VII. His great granddaughter was Elizabeth II, the present queen.

House of Hanover

EDWARD, DUKE OF KENT
(1767-1820)
Married Victoria of Saxe-Saalfield-Coburg

VICTORIA
(1819-1901)
Queen of Great Britain and Ireland 1837-1901
Married Albert of Saxe-Coburg-Gotha

VICTORIA, PRINCESS ROYAL
(1840-1901)
Married Kaiser Friedrich of Germany

ALICE, GRAND DUCHESS OF HESSE-DARMSTADT
(1843-1878)
Married Louis Grand Duke of Hesse

HELENA, PRINCESS OF SCHLESWIG-HOLSTEIN
(1846-1923)
Married Prince Christian of Schleswig-Holstein

ALBERT EDWARD VII
(1841-1910)
King of Great Britain 1901-1910
Married Princess Alexandra of Denmark

ALFRED, DUKE OF EDINBURGH
(1844-1900)
Married Grand Duchess Marie Alexandrovna of Russia

PRIME MINISTERS FROM 1837-1901

1835-41	*1841-6*	*1846-52*	*1852*	*1855-8*	*1858-9*
			EARL OF DERBY Conservative		**EARL OF DERBY** Conservative
			1852-5 **EARL OF ABERDEEN** Peelite (Supporter of Robert Peel)		*1859-65* **VISCOUNT PALMERSTON** Liberal

VISCOUNT MELBOURNE
Whig

ROBERT PEEL
Conservative

LORD JOHN RUSSELL
Liberal

VISCOUNT PALMERSTON
Liberal

RAILWAY BOOM

The map shows the growth of British railways between 1825 and 1851, which is when most of our present-day system was built. The first line was commissioned by mine owners in Darlington, and connected their mines to the port of Stockton. The next major achievement, and the start of large-scale public railways was the Liverpool to Manchester line. By 1851, trains were running throughout Britain.

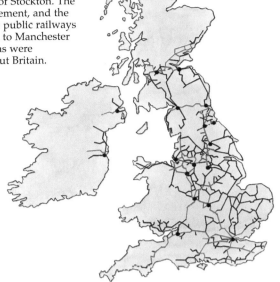

Railway key:

– – – – – – –

Stockton to
Darlington 1825

————————

Liverpool to
Manchester 1830

————————

Railway lines
by 1844

————————

Railway lines
by 1851

Museums to visit

Reconstruction of a Victorian chemist's at Blists Hill

Bethnal Green Museum of Childhood, London (toys, puppets, and dolls houses) Tel: 020 8983 5200

Big Pit Mining Museum, Torfaen, Wales (underground tours, workshops and exhibitions) Tel: 01495 790311

Blists Hill Open Air Museum, Ironbridge Gorge Museum, Ironbridge, Shropshire (50-acre working Victorian town) Tel: 01952 433522

Buckleys Yesterdays World, Battle, East Sussex (over 100,000 exhibits of domestic life from 1850-1950) Tel: 01424 775378

Reception desk inside Greater Manchester Police Station

Duke of Cornwall's Light Infantry Regiment Museum, Bodmin, Cornwall (weapons, medals, and uniforms, from 1702 to the present day) Tel: 01208 72810

Greater Manchester Police, Manchester (Victorian police station, cells, and museum) Tel: 0161 856 3287

Merseyside Maritime Museum, Liverpool (restored 19th century docks) Tel: 0151 207 0001

Noah's Ark from Museum of Childhood, Edinburgh

Museum of Childhood, Edinburgh, Scotland (toys, puzzles, books, chimney sweeps) Tel: 0131 529 4142

National Railway Museum, York (200 years of technical and social history of the railways) Tel: 01904 621261

Pump House People's History Museum, Manchester (reconstructs 200 years of social and labour history) Tel: 0161 839 6061

York Castle Museum, York (reconstructed Victorian street with stocked shops) Tel: 01904 653611

House of Coburg

ERNEST I, DUKE OF COBURG
(1784-1844)
Married Louise of Saxe-Gotha

ERNEST II, DUKE OF COBURG
(1818-1893)

ALBERT, DUKE OF SAXE-COBURG-GOTHA
(1819-1861)
Prince Consort of Great Britain and Ireland 1840-1861
Married Queen Victoria of Great Britain and Ireland

ARTHUR, DUKE OF CONNAUGHT
(1850-1942)
Married Princess Louise of Prussia

BEATRICE, PRINCESS OF BATTENBERG
(1857-1944)
Married Prince Henry of Battenberg

LOUISE, DUCHESS OF ARGYLL
(1848-1939)
Married John Campbell, Duke of Argyll

LEOPOLD, DUKE OF ALBANY
(1853-1884)
Married Princess Helena of Waldeck

WORKING PATTERNS

Industry did not start in the 19th century, but it expanded enormously, transforming Victorian Britain from an agricultural to an industrial economy. In 1801 nearly a third of the working population were employed in farming. By 1901 that figure had dropped to six per cent, and 40 per cent worked in industry. A large number worked in the service industries, such as domestic service, medicine, and banking.

Employment key:

Services   Industry   Agriculture

	1801	1841	1901
Services	32%	22%	6%
Industry	23%	34%	40%
Agriculture	45%	44%	54%

1865-6
LORD JOHN RUSSELL
Liberal

1868

1868-74

1874-80
BENJAMIN DISRAELI
Conservative

1885-6
MARQUIS OF SALISBURY
Conservative

1886-92
MARQUIS OF SALISBURY
Conservative

1894-5
5TH EARL ROSEBERY
Liberal

1866-8
EARL OF DERBY
Conservative

BENJAMIN DISRAELI
Conservative

WILLIAM EWART GLADSTONE
Liberal

1880-5
WILLIAM EWART GLADSTONE
Liberal

1886
WILLIAM EWART GLADSTONE
Liberal

1892-4
WILLIAM EWART GLADSTONE
Liberal

1895-1902
MARQUIS OF SALISBURY
Conservative

Did you know?

AMAZING FACTS

A busy Victorian railway station

The first trip organized by Thomas Cook, founder of the famous travel company, was a one-day outing from Leicester to Loughborough for a picnic in 1841. By the 1880s, he was taking people to much more exotic destinations around Europe, and even as far as Egypt.

Our phrase "in the limelight" comes from the Victorian theatre. Lights that burned lime were used as footlights at the front of the stage. They produced a very bright light, which was often used to light one of the leading characters, like a modern-day spotlight. But actors had to be careful not to get too close to these lights, otherwise they could singe, or even set fire to, the bottom of their costumes.

Victorian factory workers did not have alarm clocks to wake them up when it was time to go to work. Most workers lived close to their factory, and often the noise of the boilers or machinery starting up in the morning would be enough to wake them up. But some mines and factories employed people called "knockers-up", whose job was to bang on the workers' doors each morning to get them up for work.

Amazingly, it was only in the Victorian period that all British towns started to use the same time. Before this, each town just set its own time. It was the coming of the railways and the need to have a train timetable that worked from town to town that forced the country to adopt one standard time. The correct time was usually displayed on a public clock at the station or on the town hall, and everyone set their watches from this.

The Victorians were very modest about their bodies. Ladies in particular were careful to keep their legs covered up at all times, as allowing a gentleman to see even their ankles was considered most improper. Even to go swimming, they wore costumes with ankle length trousers.

Many of the things we associate with a typical seaside holiday come from the Victorians. They invented buckets and spades for playing on the beach, deck chairs, piers, and going for a walk along the prom. Even the ice cream cornet was frst sold in the Victorian period.

Many places around the world are named after Queen Victoria. The state of Victoria in Australia, Lake Victoria and the Victoria Falls in Africa, the city of Victoria in British Columbia, Canada, and the Victoria Mountains in New Zealand are just some of her namesakes.

At the start of Queen Victoria's reign, half of all the babies born in Britain died before they reached the age of five. The main child-killing diseases were cholera, typhoid, and diahorrea.

A popular entertainment was Buffalo Bill's Wild West Show. This four-hour spectacle starred heroes from America's Wild West – "Buffalo Bill" himself, who had earned his nickname by killing thousands of buffalo to feed the US railroad workers, along with the native American leader Big Chief Sitting Bull, and the famous sharp-shooter Annie Oakley. The show featured native American war dances, shooting displays, and an enactment of an attack on a stagecoach.

Victorian town hall clock

A poster advertising Buffalo Bill's Wild West Show

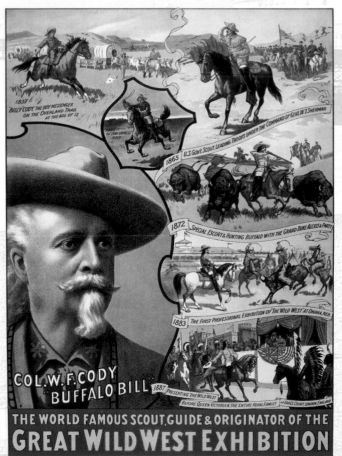

THE WORLD FAMOUS SCOUT, GUIDE & ORIGINATOR OF THE
GREAT WILD WEST EXHIBITION

QUESTIONS AND ANSWERS

Stained-glass window of Queen Victoria

Q Was Queen Victoria always popular?

A By the end of her reign, Queen Victoria was enormously popular. Her Golden and Diamond Jubilees were celebrated around the empire, and thousands of people crowded into London to watch her funeral in 1901. But not everyone liked her. She survived at least seven attempts to assassinate her, including several shootings.

Q How did Victorians show that they were in mourning?

A When someone died, close members of their family would go into a period of mourning. They wore dark, sombre clothes and special mourning jewellery, often made of a black gemstone called jet.

Q How did Victorian ladies get such big skirts?

A In the 1850s, Victorian ladies started to widen their skirts by wearing a metal cage called a crinoline. This was covered with several petticoats, and then a dress. Crinolines became wider and wider, until it was impossible for two ladies to walk through a doorway together.

A Victorian lady wearing a crinoline

Q Why was the cotton weaving industry so successful in Britain?

A From the 1770s, British cotton mills started to use new steam-powered machines. This made it quick and cheap to spin and weave cotton. The centre of the industry was in Lancashire, where the damp climate was just right for spinning the cotton threads. At one point there were 100,000 cotton looms in the Lancashire town of Burnley alone.

Q How did British soldiers get the nickname "Tommies"?

A This nickname started in the Victorian period. It came from the manual each new recruit was given in which he had to record his name, age, and other details. There was a specimen form showing how to fill in the manual, and the sample name used on this was Thomas Atkins – hence "Tommies".

Q Why did so many Victorians die from diseases like cholera and typhoid?

A At first, the Victorians had no idea that these diseases were spread by exposure to dirty drinking water and infected sewage. They believed that the diseases must be inhaled, and blamed bad-smelling air. Then in 1854, a London doctor, called John Snow, proved that a cholera outbreak had been caused by people drinking infected water from a public water pump. Public health improved dramatically when a network of new water pipes and sewers was built soon after to keep the water clean.

Record Breakers

 BIGGEST SHIPS
When Isambard Kingdom Brunel built the steam-powered *Great Western* in 1837, it was the biggest ship in the world, measuring 64.6 m from bow to stern. Brunel's later ship, the *Great Eastern*, was even bigger at 211 m in length.

 RECORD-BREAKING MONARCH
Queen Victoria was the first British queen to be photographed and filmed, and the first to have her head shown on stamps. She was queen of about one-fifth of the world, and of almost a quarter of its people.

 SUCCESS STORY
The Great Exhibition of 1851 attracted 6 million visitors and made enough profit to pay for several new museums and colleges. These included the Natural History Museum, Imperial College, and the Victoria and Albert Museum, all of which are still going strong today.

The Natural History Museum, London

Some famous Victorians

THE VICTORIAN PERIOD was an age of great change and advancement in science, the arts, industry, politics, social reform, and many other areas. So there were many, many famous Victorians – just some of them are listed here.

Statue of Thomas Hardy

WRITERS AND ARTISTS

• THE BRONTES
The Brontë sisters, Charlotte (1816–55), Emily (1818–48), and Anne (1820–49), were brought up in a remote vicarage in Yorkshire. All three of them wrote romantic novels. Their best-known books are: *Jane Eyre* (1847), written by Charlotte, *Wuthering Heights* (1847) by Emily, and *The Tenant of Wildfell Hall* (1848) by Anne.

• EDWARD BURNE-JONES (1833–98)
Painter and designer in the Pre-Raphaelite style, whose romantic paintings were often inspired by medieval tales. Burne-Jones is also famous for his tapestries and stained-glass windows for churches.

• LEWIS CARROLL (1832–98)
Carroll, whose real name was Charles Dodgson, was a mathematics lecturer at Oxford University. He wrote his famous book, *Alice's Adventures in Wonderland* (1865), for the daughter of one of his university colleagues. Carroll was also a master of nonsense verse, his best-known poem being *The Hunting of the Snark* (1876).

A scene from *A Christmas Carol*, by Dickens

• WILKIE COLLINS (1824–89)
Writer who is credited with inventing the detective novel. His most famous books are *The Woman in White* (1860) and *The Moonstone* (1868), which featured the first ever detective hero in English fiction – Sergeant Cuff.

• CHARLES DICKENS (1812–70)
The most popular novelist of the Victorian period. Most of Dickens' novels were serialized in newspapers or magazines, and he was expert at ending each episode with a cliff-hanger, so that his readers were desperate for the next episode. Dickens' best-known novels include: *The Pickwick Papers* (1836–37), *A Christmas Carol* (1843), *David Copperfield* (1849–50), and *Great Expectations* (1860–61).

• ARTHUR CONAN DOYLE (1859–1930)
Writer who is most famous for creating the detective Sherlock Holmes and his assistant, Dr Watson. Holmes first appeared in the story *A Study in Scarlet* (1887), and was a huge success with the public. In 1893, Doyle wrote a story in which Holmes was killed, but he was later forced by public demand to restore Holmes to life!

• GEORGE ELIOT (1819–80)
Novelist whose real name was Mary Ann Evans. Her most famous books include: *Adam Bede* (1859), *Mill on the Floss* (1860), and *Middlemarch* (1871–72). Eliot's early novels often focused on country life, while *Middlemarch* was a study of life in a provincial town.

• THOMAS HARDY (1840–1928)
Hardy was a novelist whose books were set in the landscape of his native Dorset. Hardy wrote about country life at a key moment, when mechanization was about to destroy ancient farming methods for ever. His most famous novels include: *Far from the Madding Crowd* (1874), *Tess of the D'Urbervilles* (1891), and *Jude the Obscure* (1895).

• WILLIAM HOLMAN HUNT (1827–1910)
Painter and member of the Pre-Raphaelite Brotherhood. Hunt's first big success was *The Light of the World* (1854), which showed Jesus knocking at the door to a human soul. Later paintings included: *The Triumph of the Innocents* (1884) and *May Morning on Magdalen Tower* (1889).

• JOHN EVERETT MILLAIS (1829–96)
Painter and founding member of the Pre-Raphaelite Brotherhood. Some of his most succesful paintings were: *The Return of the Dove to the Ark* (1851), *The Order of Release* (1853), and *The Blind Girl* (1856).

• WILLIAM MORRIS (1834–96)
Designer, craftsman, poet, and early socialist. Morris designed furniture, fabrics, wallpaper, and other decorative products, which were produced by workers using traditional techniques and handcrafting. This style became known as "Arts and Crafts" and was extremely popular.

• THE ROSETTIS
Dante Gabriel Rosetti (1828–82) was a painter and poet who helped to found the Pre-Raphaelite Brotherhood. His sister, Christina (1830–94), was also an important poet, writing ballads and love poetry in a technically advanced style.

Wallpaper designed by William Morris

PHILANTHROPISTS AND SOCIAL REFORMERS

A public water supply in 1863

• EDWIN CHADWICK (1800–90)
Doctor and leading public health reformer. In 1842, Chadwick wrote the *Report on the Sanitary Condition of the Labouring Population of Great Britain*. This was the first attempt to produce a comprehensive survey of public health. Chadwick also lead the campaign for the the first Public Health Act, which was passed in 1848.

• JOHN STUART MILL (1806–73)
Philosopher and social reformer. In *On Liberty* (1859) and other writings, Mill stated that a good government should encourage individual liberty, thus laying the basis for modern democratic government. As an MP, Mill supported women's rights, including the right to vote.

• FLORENCE NIGHTINGALE (1820–1910)
Nurse and founder of trained nursing as a profession for women. Nightingale is famous for running the field hospital at Scutari during the Crimean War, where her policies of cleanliness and good sanitation saved many soldiers' lives.

• ANNIE BESANT (1847–1933)
Campaigner whose interests included birth control, women's rights, and women's trade union rights. Besant was a defendant in a freedom of the press trial having published (with Charles Bradlaugh) *Fruits of Philosophy*, which advocated birth control. In 1888 she was involved with a strike to improve the conditions of women workers in match factories.

• JOSEPHINE BUTLER (1828–1906)
Feminist campaigner against prostitution and the exploitation of women. Butler successfully led the campaign to repeal the Contagious Diseases Acts of 1864–69, which forced prostitutes in naval and military towns to be tested for sexually transmitted diseases, when their male clients did not have to be tested.

• ELIZABETH GARRETT ANDERSON (1836–1917)
The first woman to qualify as doctor in Britain (1865) and the first woman member of the British Medical Association (1873–92). London's Elizabeth Garrett Anderson Hospital was named after her.

• KEIR HARDIE (1856–1915)
Socialist and labour leader. In 1892, Hardie was elected to parliament as an independent candidate – the first MP to represent working men and women. In 1893 he founded the Independent Labour Party, the forerunner of the modern-day Labour Party.

• OCTAVIA HILL (1838–1912)
Social reformer who was particularly involved in slum clearance and building better houses for the poor.

• LORD SHAFTESBURY (1801–85)
Factory reformer. Shaftesbury was an MP who campaigned for better conditions for working people. He was responsible for the 1842 Mines Act, which banned women, girls, and boys under the age of 10 from working in coal mines, and for the 1847 "Ten Hours Act", which shortened the working day in textile mills to 10 hours. Shaftesbury also set up the "ragged schools" (see p. 24).

Bust of Florence Nightingale

ENGINEERS AND INVENTORS

• ALEXANDER GRAHAM BELL (1847–1922)
Inventor of the telephone. Bell was born in Scotland, but later moved to the USA. He became interested in the idea of transmitting sound by electricity and in 1876 patented the first telephone. Later, Bell continued his experiments in many diverse areas – the phonograph, aerial vehicles, and teaching speech to the deaf.

Manufacturing Bessemer steel

• HENRY BESSEMER (1813–98)
Inventor and engineer who developed the Bessemer process – a fast, cheap way to manufacture steel in large quantities.

• JESSE BOOT (1850–1931)
English drug manufacturer, and founder of the Boots chain store. Boot opened his first shop in Nottingham in 1877, and by mass-selling at low prices effectively started the chain store. In 1892 he began large-scale drug manufacture.

• ISAMBARD KINGDOM BRUNEL (1806–59)
One of the greatest Victorian engineers. Brunel created the Great Western Railway and designed the Clifton Suspension Bridge in Bristol. He also built three record-breaking ships: the *Great Western* (1837) which was the first trans-Atlantic steamship, the *Great Britain* (1843) which was the first screw-propelled steamship, and the *Great Eastern* (1858).

• JOHN BOYD DUNLOP (1840–1921)
Inventor of the pneumatic tyre (1887). In 1889, Dunlop formed the Dunlop Rubber Company to manufacture pneumatic bicycle tyres.

• WILLIAM FOX TALBOT (1800–77)
Pioneer photographer. In 1840 he invented an early form of photograph, called the calotype. In 1844–46 Fox Talbot published *The Pencil of Nature*, the first book to be illustrated with photographs.

A "mousetrap" camera from 1835, as used by Fox Talbot

Find out more

IN BRITAIN, WE ARE surrounded by reminders of the Victorian period. You will probably be able to spot some Victorian houses and other buildings close to where you live, or streets with names like "Victoria", "Albert", "Wellington", or "Gladstone", which usually have a Victorian connection. Another good way to find out more about our Victorian ancestors is to visit a museum. Some of the most famous museums are listed here and on p. 43, but your local museum may well have a Victorian collection that is worth visiting.

AROUND YOUR TOWN
Most British towns have a wealth of Victorian buildings. Some of these are public buildings, such as town halls, schools, or churches, others are mills, factories, or other industrial buildings. The Victorians also left behind many statues of famous people – politicians, military leaders, and, of course, of Queen Victoria herself. So have a scout around, and see what Victorian treasures you can spot in your town.

This statue of Queen Victoria stands outside Windsor Castle.

VISIT A MUSEUM
Some museums, such as the Victoria and Albert Museum in London, have big collections of objects and clothes from the Victorian period. There are also museums, such as Queen Street Mill in Burnley or the Great Western Railway Museum in Swindon, where you can see Victorian industrial equipment in action. Or you could look round some Victorian houses at the Blists Hill Victorian Museum in Telford or the Museum of Welsh Life, outside Cardiff.

The Victoria and Albert Museum, in London

A terrace of Victorian houses

VICTORIAN HOUSES

If you live in a British town, you probably live near a street like this one, lined with terraces of Victorian houses. You may even live in a Victorian house yourself. Some typical features of Victorian houses to look out for are: a big bay window at the front, sash windows (windows that push up and down), and the use of different coloured bricks for decoration.

FAMOUS LANDMARKS

Many of Britain's most famous buildings are Victorian. For example, the Lancashire town of Blackpool became a popular seaside resort during the Victorian period, and the tower, piers, and other landmarks were all built at this time. Some other famous Victorian buildings you might spot are listed in the "Places to Visit" box.

USEFUL WEBSITES

General information about the Victorian era, including architecture, daily life, museums, and events
www.victorianstation.com

History of the Victorian period
www.britainexpress.com/History/Victorian

Queen Victoria and the royal family
www.royal.gov.uk/history/victoria

Website for the Victoria and Albert Museum
www.vam.ac.uk

Blackpool Tower

IN YOUR OWN HOME

Can openers, vacuum cleaners, electric irons, and kettles are just some of the useful items around your home that were invented by the Victorians. Even flushing toilets were first installed in people's houses during this period, so you can thank the Victorians that you don't have to visit an earth closet at the bottom of your garden!

An early flushing toilet, from the Victorian period

Places to Visit

THE VICTORIA AND ALBERT MUSEUM, LONDON
Founded in the Victorian period, this museum contains a huge collection of porcelain, tapestries, jewellery, glass, clothes, paintings, and photographs from all over the world. Star Victorian exhibits include:
• The Morris, Gamble, and Poynter rooms, decorated by the three designers themselves, who recreated historic styles using the modern materials of the industrial age.

QUEEN STREET MILL, BURNLEY
At the only remaining steam-powered cotton mill in Britain, visitors can see the 500-horsepower steam engine and the weaving looms in action.

ARNLEY MILLS MUSEUM, LEEDS
A 19th century woollen mill, which contains working looms.

THE MUSEUM OF WELSH LIFE, ST FAGANS, OUTSIDE CARDIFF
This open-air museum is home to more than 40 original buildings that have been moved from all over Wales. Victorian attractions include:
• a bakehouse where bread and cakes are still cooked daily
• a grocery shop
• a rural school
• a terrace of iron workers' cottages.

SS GREAT BRITAIN, GREAT WESTERN DOCK, BRISTOL
The *SS Great Britain*, designed by Brunel, was the world's first large iron passenger ship. The wreckage of the ship is now being restored in the Bristol dock where it was originally built.

SALTAIRE, NEAR BRADFORD
This model industrial village, completed in 1873, was built by Sir Titus Salt to house the workers employed in his textile mill.

SOME FAMOUS VICTORIAN BUILDINGS TO SEE:
Here are just a few examples of Victorian architecture from around the country. There are plenty more!
• The Houses of Parliament, St Pancras Station, The Albert Memorial, and the Natural History Museum, all in London
• The Rotunda and the Museum of Science and Industry, Manchester
• Blackpool Tower and piers
• Brighton piers
• The Clifton Suspension Bridge, Bristol
• The town hall and shopping arcades, Leeds.
• The Forth Rail Bridge, outside Edinburgh
• The Scott Monument, Edinburgh
• Cardiff Castle

Victorian doll

Glossary

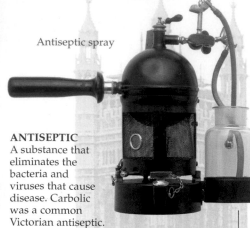

Antiseptic spray

ANTISEPTIC
A substance that eliminates the bacteria and viruses that cause disease. Carbolic was a common Victorian antiseptic.

ARTS AND CRAFTS MOVEMENT A group of artists and architects with a passion for decorative handicrafts, who sought to revive medieval craftsmanship.

BACK-TO-BACK HOUSING Two rows of terraced houses built facing away from each other, so that their back walls are adjacent or separated by a narrow alley.

BALLOT The total votes cast in an election to select a representative, or group of representatives.

BANK HOLIDAYS Several weekdays throughout the year on which banks are closed by law and which are observed as national holidays.

BRITISH EMPIRE Territories all over the world that were controlled by Britain.

CHARTISM A movement (1836–48) set up to achieve certain political reforms, such as the right to vote for all adults and the introduction of secret ballots.

CHOLERA A highly infectious disease that causes severe diarrhoea and vomiting, and often kills. Cholera is caught by consuming contaminated water or food.

CLASS A group of people sharing a similar social rank.

COLONIALISM The practice of a powerful country extending control over other countries or states. It can also be called imperialism.

COLONY An area that has been occupied by settlers from another, more powerful country, and is now ruled from that country.

CONSTITUTIONAL MONARCH A king or queen who is the head of state, but holds no power to govern their country. Real power is in the hands of a democratically elected government.

CORONATION The ceremony to crown a king or queen.

COTTAGE INDUSTRY A business activity that is carried out at home. Before the Industrial Revolution, work such as spinning and weaving cloth was often done in people's homes.

ECONOMY The management of a country's finances and activities concerned with the production, distribution, and consumption of goods and services.

EMIGRATION Leaving one's home country permanently to settle in another country.

ETIQUETTE Rules on how people are expected to dress and behave in social situations.

Tiles designed by the Pre-Raphaelite artist, William Morris

EXPLOITATION The practice of taking advantage of another person or group of people for one's own benefit.

FIELD HOSPITAL A temporary hospital set up near a battlefield to treat soldiers who are wounded in the fighting.

FINE ARTS Arts such as poetry, music, painting, and sculpture.

FINISHED GOODS Items that have been manufactured in a factory.

FOUNDRY A factory where metal ore is melted down, purified, and cast into objects.

GOTHIC A style of architecture, featuring the use of pointed arches, that was popular in Western Europe from the 12th to the 16th centuries.

HOME RULE The freedom of a country to govern itself.

INDUSTRIAL REVOLUTION The changes that took place in Britain and other countries during the 18th and 19th centuries as a result of industrialization.

INDUSTRIALIZATION The development of industries, such as steel-making and weaving, which used factories with power-driven machinery on an extensive scale.

JINGOISM An extreme form of nationalism.

LITERACY The ability to read and write.

MASS PRODUCTION Large-scale production of goods, usually carried out in a factory.

MECHANIZATION The equipping of industry with machines.

Back-to-back houses in Hebden Bridge, Yorkshire

MIDDLE CLASS The class of people who earned their living from working in the professions, such as teaching, medicine, or the law, or from owning businesses.

MILL A factory where cotton and wool are spun into thread and then woven to make cloth.

MISSIONARY A member of an organization undertaking religious or charitable works, often with the aim of converting other people to their faith.

MUNICIPAL BUILDING A building that has been provided by local government for public use, such as a town hall or library.

NEW MODEL DWELLINGS Sanitary and comfortable homes for working class people, built by the Victorian philanthropist George Peabody and others.

Looms in a mill from the Victorian period

OLD TORY A member of the political party that supported the power of the monarch.

PATRIOTISM Devotion to one's own country and concern for its defence.

PENNY-DREADFUL A cheap, often sensational, book or magazine.

PENNY-FARTHING BICYCLE An early bicycle with a large front wheel and a small back one, with the pedals on the front wheel.

PHILANTHROPY The practice of performing charitable or generous actions to people in a less fortunate social position than oneself.

PLANTATION A large estate on which one crop, such as tea, sugar, or tobacco, is grown. In colonial times, plantations were often owned by colonists and worked by poorly paid local people, or even slaves.

PRE-RAPHAELITE BROTHERHOOD The association of painters and writers, founded in 1848, that revived the vivid and realistic use of colour considered typical of Italian painting before the 16th century artist Raphael.

PUBLIC AMENITIES Buildings and places that are open to every one and help to make life in a town more pleasant. Parks, libraries, museums, and swimming pools are all public amenities.

QUAKER A member of a Christian group devoted to peaceful principles. Quakers do not have a formal set of beliefs or ordained ministers. Their acts of worship are often based around silence.

RANGE A large cooking stove on which the burners and ovens are kept permanently hot.

RAW MATERIALS The materials used to make manufactured goods. For example, cotton and wool are the raw materials from which cloth is made.

RURAL To do with the countryside.

SAFETY BICYCLE A bicycle with two same-sized wheels, driven round by pedals and a chain. It was the forerunner of the bicycles we use today.

SANITATION The safe disposal of sewage and refuse and the supply of clean, running water to people's houses. Sanitation was a problem, because towns did not have proper sewer systems and many houses did not have toilets.

SCULLERY A room, situated at the back of a house, where dishes and clothes were washed in a sink.

SLATE A small, flat piece of slate stone, often framed with wood, used for writing on. Victorian children used slates instead of writing paper at school.

SLUMS The squalid part of a city, full of overcrowded houses in poor condition.

SOCIALIST A person who believes that society should be organized to benefit everyone in it, not just rich and powerful people. This might involve providing free schools and health services, and public ownership of transport and other services.

SPINNING JENNY A machine for spinning cotton or wool on to more than one spindle at a time.

SPINNING MULE A kind of spinning machine invented in 1779 by Samuel Crompton. It could spin up to 1,000 threads on to spindles at a time.

TENEMENT BUILDING A large building divided into a number of rooms or flats.

A penny-farthing bicycle

TERRACED HOUSES A row of houses that are joined together by their side walls.

TEXTILE A woven fabric or cloth.

THREE R'S The three basic subjects that were taught in Victorian schools – reading, writing, and arithmetic.

TRADE UNION An association of workers whose aim is to improve their pay and working conditions.

TRUCK SYSTEM A system sometimes used by Victorian factory owners which forced workers to accept payment of their wages in goods, rather than money.

TYPHOID an extremely infectious disease that gives the sufferer high fever, spots, and stomach ache. It is caused by eating contaminated food or by drinking contaminated water. Typhoid is short for "typhoid fever".

Cotton textiles

UPPER CLASS The wealthiest and most privileged class of people, consisting mostly of the aristocracy. Members of the upper class usually did not have to work to earn their living.

URBAN To do with towns.

VICTORIAN PERIOD The period of British history corresponding to the reign of Queen Victoria (1837–1901).

WATER FRAME A device for spinning cotton invented in 1771 by Richard Arkwright. It used power from a water wheel to work all the spinning machines in a mill.

WHIG A member of the political party that opposed the power of the monarch.

WORKHOUSE A place where people who were too poor to support themselves and their families were sent. They received food and lodging in return for doing work, but conditions were very harsh.

WORKING CLASS The class of people who earned their living from manual or industrial work, such as farm labourers, factory workers, or servants.

Eyewitness titles in this series:

Whale

Horse

Insect

Knight

Mammal

Mummy

Plant

Pond & River

Seashore

Shakespeare

Shipwreck

Victorians

**Future titles
to include:**

Arms & Armour

Dance

Dinosaur

Early People

Explorer

Flying Machine

Fossil

Invention

Jungle

Ocean

Index

Acknowledgements

Dorling Kindersley would like to thank:
Gary Ombler for photographic assistance; Blists Hill and Jackfield Tile Museum; The Ironbridge Gorge Museum, especially Rachel Ilisse, Dennis Jones, Martin Harris, Traci Dix- Williams, and Stefanie Higgins; The Museum of London, especially Peter Jennings, Alex Werner, and Karen Fielder; Victoria Haywood-Dunne, and Marianne Petrou for revisions; Carol Davis for art-editing the jacket.

The publisher would also like to thank the following for their kind permission to reproduce their photographs:

KEY
a = above, b = bottom, c = centre, f = far, l = left, r = right, t = top.

AKG London: 66bl

Bodleian Library, Oxford (N.12288b): 54–55; Tim Booth 681 Bridgeman Art Library: 20c, 32c;
William Drummond, London 10c; Stapleton Collection 15cr; Tretyakov Gallery, Moscow 12cl; York City Art Gallery 27tr; National Gallery Scotland, Edinburgh 33b; Fitzwilliam Museum, University of Cambridge 37br
Corbis: 15tc, 17cr, 26b, 36c, 38br Joe Cornish 70b
Dickens House: 28c; ET Archive 32bl, 33tr; Tate Gallery 27tl, 27cl; LSE 39br
Edifice: Gillian Darley 69tl; Lewis-Darley 68r
Mary Evans Picture Library: 9cb, 9tr, 11tr, 12br, 12tc, 16bl, 17tr, 19tc, 23cra, 24bl, 27bl, 28tr, 29tl, 29tc, 29br, 29bl, 29bc, 31tr, 31c, 37c, 37tl, 37tc, 39tr, 40bl, 41tl, 41cla, 41c, 41br, 43br, 67tl
Fine Art Photographs: 13tr, 34c
Getty Images: 18tr, 19tr, 22cr, 28tl, 28bl, 31c, 32cl

Ironbridge Gorge Museum 68Bkg
Jarrold Publishing: 43t
London Transport Museum: 13cal
Museum of Childhood: 43cra
Museum of London: 25tr, 31tl
Natural History Museum, London: 37cr, 37c, 65br
National Museum of Scotland: Edinburgh United Services Museum: 39tl
National Portrait Gallery: 8c, 42l
Stephen Oliver: 64tr, 66Bkg
Rex Features: 41tr
The Royal Collection. Her Majesty the Queen: Endpapers
Royal Geographic Society: 37cra; Royal Green Jackets Museum: 39c
Sotheby's Picture Library: 11bl, 18bl, 18c
Science Museum: 15br, 15bl, 30bc, 30br, 31bl, 31br, 68cb, 69cb
Science & Society Picture Library: 14cl, 14br, 15tr; Science Museum: 33cl, 33cr, 67bl; NMPFT 67br
Trip:/R. Kuehn: 40c.

Jacket:
Front: **The Bridgeman Art Library:** Museum of London, UK tc, The Royal Collection © 2011 Her Majesty Queen Elizabeth II b. **Dorling Kindersley:** The Museum of London tr (hat), ftr. *Back:* **Dorling Kindersley:** Blists Hill Museum, Ironbridge, Shropshire bl, The Museum of London bc.

Wallchart:
DK Images: Blists Hill Museum, Ironbridge, Shropshire cla, clb; Mark Hall Cycle Museum, Harlow Council tr; Natural History Museum, London crb (notebook), crb (orange butterfly); Science Museum, London cra (kettle); **Mary Evans Picture Library:** c, ftl

All other images © Dorling Kindersley. For further information see:
www.dkimages.com